PHAEDO

The Library of Liberal Arts
OSKAR PIEST, FOUNDER

PHAEDO

PLATO

Translated by
F. J. CHURCH

With an introduction by
FULTON H. ANDERSON

· ·

The Library of Liberal Arts
published by

BOBBS-MERRILL EDUCATIONAL PUBLISHING
Indianapolis

The Bobbs-Merrill Company, Inc.
4300 West 62nd Street
Indianapolis, Indiana 46268

First Edition
Seventeenth Printing—1981
Library of Congress Catalog Card Number: 51—10496
ISBN 0–672–60192–3 (pbk.)

CONTENTS

SELECTED BIBLIOGRAPHY

Anderson, F. H., *The Argument of Plato*. London, 1934, pp. 114-21, 186-90.

Archer-Hind, R.D., *The Phaedo of Plato*. London, 1883.

Burnet, J., *Greek Philosophy*, Part I. Oxford, 1913, Chapters IX-X
————— *Plato's Phaedo*. Oxford, 1911.

Church, F. J., *The Trial and Death of Socrates*. London, 1923, pp. ix-lxxxix.

Fraser, J. G., *The Growth of Plato's Ideal Theory*. London, 1930, pp. 54-71.

Gaye, R. K., *The Platonic Conception of Immortality and Its Connection with the Theory of Ideas*. London, 1904.

Geddes, W. D., *The Phaedo of Plato*. London, 1885.

Grote, G., *Plato and the Other Companions of Socrates*. London 1867, Vol. II, pp. 152-205.

Prüm, E., *Der Phaidon über Wesen und Bestimmung des Menschen*. Archiv. f. Gesch. d. Philos., XXI, 1908, pp. 30-49.

Shorey, P., *What Plato Said*. Chicago, 1933, pp. 169-84, 523-37.

Stewart, J. A., *The Myths of Plato*. London, 1905, pp. 77-111.

Taylor, A. E., *Plato the Man and His Work*. New York, 1936, pp. 174-208.

Williamson, H., *The Phaedo of Plato*. London, 1904.

INTRODUCTION

Plato's *Phaedo* is the record of Socrates' last day on earth. The scene is an Athenian prison in the summer of 399 B.C. The dialogue concerns the nature and functions of the human soul. The argument which proceeds with ease is broken here and there by touches of humor and passages of moral eloquence. Throughout the day there are reminders of approaching tragedy, as when the jailer removes the chains from Socrates' legs, when he advises Socrates not to heat himself by discussion—otherwise a dose of poison larger than usual will have to be prepared—and when he arrives finally for the execution. As the portrayal of the end of a good, wise, and just man, who dies without fear, thoughtful of others, and sensitive to the sorrow of his friends, the beauty and poignancy of the *Phaedo* are probably unmatched in the history of human literature.

Socrates has been the author's teacher. Plato is twenty-eight when Socrates dies; he has known him for some years. The pupil is born to high station. The master is a stone-cutter. Between 432 B.C. and 422 B.C. he serves as a soldier. On campaigns his fellows are amazed at his courage and resistance to hunger and cold. Later he becomes well known as an intrepid individual who refuses to obey the order of reigning political tyrants to deliver a political opponent of theirs into their hands for execution. In physical appearance Socrates is unprepossessing to the point of grotesqueness, with a flat nose, protruding eyes, and awkward gait. He has an infectious ironic mirth and his perception of thoughts and persons is instantaneous. All sorts of people seek his company; many are impressed, some remain his disciples; others, like Critias and Alcibiades, find his sayings too difficult for practice and fall away.

In most of Plato's dialogues Socrates is the chief *dramatis persona*. Usually he has the rôle of interrogator who invites and

comments on the opinions of others. But in the *Symposium,
Apology, Crito,* and *Phaedo* he proclaims and elaborates his own
convictions concerning good and evil, life and death. The first
of these four is a drinking party. Here he appears among gay
and carefree friends in full lustiness of life. The other three,
with sharp contrast of scene, show him on trial, in prison, and
about to undergo execution.

In the *Apology* two charges are laid by his accusers: (1)
Socrates has introduced strange gods to Athens; (2) Socrates
corrupts the Athenian young. The indictments are not sincere;
the real reason for the prosecution has been withheld. Socrates
has consistently castigated his fellow citizens, notably the poli-
ticians, poets, orators, and artisans, for their inexpertness in
distinguishing between sham and truth and their failure to pursue
honest inquiry into the nature of justice. (His public accusers
are significantly a politician, a poet, and a rhetorician.) The
second formal indictment reminds the jury—and this is undoubtedly the intention behind it—that Critias and Alcibiades are two
persons who have been attracted to Socrates; and the former of
these has been among the city's tyrants who have lately been
removed from office, and the latter has proved himself a profaner
of the "mysteries" and a political renegade and traitor to his city.

As for the first indictment: any reflective thinker who undertakes the task of bringing a degree of consistency into the varied
and complex mythological stories about manifold Greek deities
will undoubtedly be deemed guilty of something or other. Moreover, Socrates has been in the habit of speaking of a "demon"
which has possessed him. This "inner voice," he explains, has
warned him against action when he might have done wrong, and
has admonished him when advising others.

Socrates as an honest man denies the charges. He proceeds
before the jury to compare himself to a gadfly whose function
has been the arousing of Athenians from their complacent acceptance of unfounded opinions. He taunts his hearers with the claim
that, like a victorious Olympic competitor, he should be kept at
public expense. He is found guilty and sentenced to death.

The sentence cannot be put into effect immediately. The verdict has been rendered the day after the sacred ship has been sent on a mission in annual commemoration of the voyage of Theseus to Crete, and no one may be legally executed until she returns. The trip in this instance takes thirty days.

At dawn of the day on which the ship is to reach Athens, Crito—in a brief dialogue which bears his name—visits Socrates in prison and requests him to escape and flee to friends in Thessaly. Crito has "influence." He, along with Cebes and Simmias, is prepared to provide whatever funds may be required. Socrates refuses to go. The law, administered as it is by erring men, may be wronging him; he will not detract from its worth. The observance and the operation of law, Socrates reflects, provide order and stability in societies. Laws are like parents. Living under their ministration and protection implies the acceptance of a moral contract which enjoins obedience. The laws have found him guilty. The day for his execution has dawned; the sacred ship has completed her voyage. Socrates will accept the penalty exacted by his political peers.

His wife and the youngest of his three children are with him when the prison opens in the morning—it would seem that they have been with him through the night. His wife is overwrought and goes home, to return in the afternoon accompanied by other women of the household. With compassion Socrates persuades them to leave before the final hour. On these intimate family meetings Plato is fittingly silent. The remainder of the day is spent with friends and philosophical inquirers in conversation about the soul, its nature, and its immortality. Phaedo, who is present, describes the scene to Echecrates at Phlius. Phaedo is a native of Elis. At one time he had been taken prisoner in a military campaign and brought to Athens as a slave. He was ransomed and became an intimate disciple of Socrates. On the death of his master he returns to his native city to become the founder of the Elean school of philosophy. It is highly probable that the account of Socrates' last day which is recorded in the

dialogue which bears his name, is given on his way back home
to a group of Pythagoreans. Of these only Echecrates is men-
tioned by name. He is placed by Diogenes Laertius among "the
last of the Pythagoreans."

Persons with Socrates in the prison are the Athenians—
Antisthenes, Apollodorus, Critobulus, Crito, Hermogenes, Epigenes, Aeschines, Ctesippus, and Menexenus; three Thebans—Cebes,
Simmias, and Phaidondas; two Megarians—Euclides and Terpsion. Aristippus and Cleombrotus have not learned of the ship's
return in time to get back from Aegina before the execution.
Plato is unable to attend because of illness.

Of these, Apollodorus, whom Plato makes the narrator in the
Symposium, is an impulsive person, greatly attached to Socrates,
yet petulant and given—as effeminate men sometimes are—to
telling slanderous tales about others. Along with Antisthenes he
belongs to the Cynic group within the Socratic circle. Critobulus
is a prepossessing young man, a little too disposed to rely on his
good looks and pleasing manners for ingratiating himself with
others. He is with his father Crito. This man is wealthy, fearless,
and highly respected throughout Athens for his honesty and
integrity. Crito is Socrates' oldest and staunchest friend. He has
given financial surety that Socrates will not leave prison when
allowed access to his friends. And yet so great is his belief in
Socrates' worth to Athens and to the Greek world generally, that
he is prepared to accept heavy financial responsibility if Socrates
will leave the prison and go to another city. He is the friend
who is closeted with Socrates while the latter makes his final
preparations for drinking the poison which will bring death.
While he has tried to convince Socrates that he should refuse to
undergo the final penalty, he now defers in modesty to Socrates'
decision in the matter.

Hermogenes is a younger brother of Callias who, according
to Plato, has spent more money on Sophists than any contemporary. Both brothers are members of the larger Socratic circle.
Epigenes is interested in philosophy, but inclined to laziness.
Aeschines is a writer of philosophic dialogues. Antisthenes is the

leader of the Cynic group. Ctesippus, who appears in the *Euthy-
demus* and the *Lysis*, is a person "of gentle birth and breeding,"
and displays "a certain violence of youth." Menexenus, after
whom a Platonic dialogue is called, is a scion of a family long
dominant in Athenian politics. He regards himself as one necessarily consigned to a political career.

Euclides and Terpsion, who hail from Megara, are enthusiastic
exponents of Eleatic doctrines. Of Aristippus many conjectures
are entertained and few facts are known. It seems that his
experience of life is wide and he is an avowed Hedonist. A person
called Cleombrotus is said to have thrown himself into the sea
after reading Plato's *Phaedo*. Whether the story itself is well
founded and whether it concerns the Cleombrotus who appears
in this dialogue are questions to which no authoritative answer
can be given.

Of Phaidondas nothing is known except his loyalty to Socrates. The other two Thebans, Cebes and Simmias, are disciples
of the Pythagorean Philolaus. In the present dialogue they are
the chief interlocutors of Socrates, and as a consequence the
dramatic argument comes to have a Pythagorean setting. The
reader, of course, will not conclude because of this that the doctrines set forth by Socrates are consequentially Pythagorean.
Indeed, what the contemporary teachings of the Pythagoreans
are is exceedingly difficult to descry. The cult which traditionally
bears this name has spread and separated in varied ways. Some
of its numbers are interested in distinctive religious ordinances;
others seek definition and system in mathematics; a third group
which includes Cebes and Simmias concern themselves with
physical theories. Yet most, if not all their number, remain
aware of the two tenets entertained in the original school; namely,
that the soul transmigrates from body to body, and that knowledge in this world is reminiscence of objects earlier cognized in
an intelligible realm of Forms.

The list of persons within the dialogue is imposing in its
variety. Athenians of many interests and philosophers of several
persuasions have been stirred by Socrates' condemnation and

approaching execution. Moreover, the preoccupations and doctrines which the author on this occasion brings under review are
highly significant. This latter fact requires some emphasis, in
that not a few historians are disposed to represent Socrates as a
person who, while intelligent and inquisitive, confines his thinking up to the age of seventy to questions about definition and a
simple sort of induction in the realm of ethics. For this view a
reliance upon certain sayings of Xenophon and on slight Aristotelian commentary is largely responsible.

The sources for a knowledge of Socrates' life and teachings
are mainly four: (a) the caricatures of Aristophanes, (b) the
Memorabilia and other writings of Xenophon, (c) the dialogues
of Plato, and (d) the works of Aristotle. The last of these four
authors reports that Socrates is the originator of definition and
induction, and remarks that the Socratic doctrine of Forms is
allied to the Pythagorean theory of numbers. But Aristotle
was not born until fifteen years after Socrates' death; and he is
disposed to choose from the opinions of his predecessors only
such as will suit his preoccupations.

Xenophon, who undertakes a "defense" of Socrates, does not
understand his hero. He has spent relatively little time with
Socrates, and he is away on military duty during Socrates' last
years. Were Socrates as innocuous as Xenophon represents him
to be, he never could have drawn reflective people about him,
nor have dominated the mind of Plato, nor indeed have been
made the object of persecution by his fellow Athenians.

Aristophanes is a writer of understanding and a close acquaintance of Socrates. His *Clouds,* in which Socrates is caricatured, is quoted in the *Symposium* as a tribute to the philosopher. Socrates is portrayed by Aristophanes in the *Clouds* as
a physical inquirer.

In the *Phaedo* those who question and listen to Socrates
assume that he is familiar with the cosmological and physical
theories of the Milesians, Heracliteans, Eleatics, Empedocleans,
Pythagoreans, and with the writings on medicine and music. And,
most significantly, Plato's account of the solution of the major

problems raised in the dialogue depends upon the transition within the mind of Socrates from an earlier concern with physical causation to a later inquiry into the nature of logical cause and essence.

Allowing for some dramatic amplification by the author, the *Phaedo* may be taken as a faithful account of Socrates' concerns and conversation during his last hours on earth. Certain of those present in the prison, including Euclides and Terpsion, were still alive when the piece was written. Plato was absent, but there can be no doubt that he received an accurate report of what went on.

The main topic for discussion in the dialogue is the soul's immortality. This theme is introduced with the observation by Socrates that the philosopher does not fear death with its separation of soul from body, because during his life he has undergone an abnegation of the lusts and confusions which beset the embodied soul and has made his escape to a realm of abiding things beyond the vicissitudes of change and decay. Even as the philosopher has found in wisdom a purification, so will he welcome death as the final step in an initiation into true being. It has been taught by Philolaus the Pythagorean that persons while inhabiting this world are in ward and should not force the doors of their prison. Socrates finds this reasoning difficult to follow, but he thinks that man is in some sense a chattel of the gods and therefore should not take his own life, but await their call in good time. Cebes and others of the company are hoping that Socrates will give a reasoned defense for his profession of immortality, the more especially because there is a current belief that the human soul is no more than physical breath which death disperses.

This "proof" is begun by way of analogy. Opposites pass into opposites. When a thing becomes hotter it becomes so from what is colder; the colder becomes from the hotter. The greater becomes from the lesser, and the lesser from the greater. Sleeping passes into waking, waking into sleeping. By the same token death comes from life and life from death. Again, a composite thing is more liable to dissolution than one which is incomposite. What is composed of parts may be deemed prone to decomposition. Many objects of this sort are seen to be incessantly in change and varying continuously in appearance. Others, like Forms or Ideas, which belong to the intelligible realm and not the visible, and which are perceived not by sense but in intellectual understanding, prove to be unvarying, changeless, and indissoluble. Of these two sorts the body has kinship with the former, and the soul with the latter.

Cebes recalls an argument which Socrates is reported to favor. This is to the effect that on the presentation of appropriate diagrams an untutored observer will recognize universal geometric truths. He does not "see" the latter but only particular figures inadequately drawn—the inscribed square or triangle is rarely drawn to specification; its lines are not straight nor its angles of proper dimensions—yet on their presentation to his visual sense he is enabled to cognize such intellectual objects as squareness and triangularity. Since these have not been taught him nor seen by his eye, it may be concluded that his perception of them is really a recollection of things already known. This doctrine, that knowledge is reminiscence, is illustrated by Socrates' instruction of a slave boy in an earlier dialogue of Plato's, the *Meno*. It rests on the hypothesis that while inhabiting an intelligible realm in a previous mode of existence the soul has been in direct contact with Forms. On its entry to the present world the soul is enclosed in a body and is consequently rendered subject to the darkness of sense and the disturbance of physical appetite. It forgets the objects which it has formerly entertained. On the occasion of the presentation of particulars it is reminded of the Forms which it has already known and through memory it recognizes them.

The last argument is enough for most of the company, but not for Simmias or Cebes. Evidence for the soul's pre-existence is not proof of its survival in perpetuity. May it not be, asks Simmias, that the soul puts on successive bodies like a person puts on his garments, and finally one day wears his last garment and dies? Or, again, adds Cebes, may there not be soundness in a current hypothesis that the soul is nothing more than a "harmony" or organization of bodily elements which, when brought into a certain conjunction, constitute an organism, and, if so, would not the soul cease to be when these were decomposed? To use the term *harmonia* in its musical sense—for it means both conjunction and musical mode—can a harmony remain after the strings of the lyre are broken?

Echecrates voices the dismay of the listeners at these queries. Socrates is not perturbed. He warns the company against misology. Misanthropy, the hatred of men, and misology, the hatred of ideas, spring from disappointment after the placing of too great confidence in persons and discourses. Few people are bad, few good; most are morally mediocre. If discussion sometimes disappoints, reason is not to blame but the inexpertness of the argument. As for the soundness of the description of the soul in terms of harmony which Simmias has adduced: a mode of musical harmony is a mode and nothing different; it cannot manifest degrees of better or worse as a determined way of making melody or ordering sounds. An adjustment of physical parts to the making of a specific totality suffers the same limitations. But souls vary with respect to degrees of good and evil. If one were to construe the soul's virtue in terms of "harmony," as is sometimes done, and at the same time were to accept the thesis in question, he would find it necessary to posit a second harmony within the original harmony, and thus doubly to complicate his difficulties. The concept "harmony" is unfortunate for further reasons. A harmony cannot run counter to the parts of which it is a harmony; but the soul in its operations masters the body and frustrates appetites which are occasioned by the body's presence. A description of the soul's nature as a mechanical adjustment among physical parts fails to take under reckoning the soul's possession and use of those innate ideas which Cebes has admitted to the satisfaction of Simmias into an earlier account of knowing.

The second difficulty, voiced by Cebes, is not easily met. It raises a major question of causation, and presents a problem which Socrates has long considered. When a young man, Socrates set out with great enthusiasm to investigate nature and to find out why things become what they do. He considered such questions as these: Is growth the result of fermentation by heat and cold?

Is blood the element by which we think, or is this air, or fire, or something else? Is the brain the organ of hearing, sight, and smell? Do memory and opinion come from these, and is knowledge founded on the memory and opinion which thus ensue? In his preoccupation with such inquiries he not only forgot what he had previously known, but he became thoroughly confused by the opinions he had gathered.

While in despair he heard someone reading from a book by Anaxagoras the statement that Mind is the cause of all things. He now thought his difficulties would be resolved on finding, as he hoped, reasons for things being what they are. But to his disappointment he discovered that Anaxagoras, like others before, had so completely accounted for the world by the activities of air, ether, water, and other absurdities, that there was no place left for the Mind he had asserted to be the explanation of all. His conclusion was like someone saying that the cause of Socrates' being in prison and not on his way to Boeotia is that his bones and muscles do not carry him there.

Anaxagoras having failed him, Socrates turned to what he ironically calls a "second best" explanation of cause. This, in brief, is to the effect that the reason for a thing's being or becoming what it is, is due to its participation in Forms or Ideas. Suppose, for example, that Simmias who is small becomes great, or what is one becomes two. Smallness in the one case does not become greatness, nor does oneness in the other become twoness. The Forms (or classes or predicates), of which smallness, greatness, oneness, and twoness are examples, never themselves change. When what is called change takes place in an object, that which is discerned to change ceases to participate in one Form and takes on another. Change in a subject is marked by a succession of predicates, but not by the transformation of any predicate into another. An object is seen to "move" or become when it ceases to participate in one Form and afterward participates in another Form.

Now there are Forms which are mere accidents: Simmias may remain Simmias while he increases his stature in passing from smallness to greatness. But there are also Forms which constitute the essential natures of objects. To illustrate: where one finds fire there is always hotness. Fire participates in hotness, as snow does in coldness. Fire will not admit coldness, nor snow hotness. The numbers three and five admit oddness but not evenness. Oddness is essential to them. To apply this aspect of the doctrine of Forms to the essentiality of the soul: even as fire cannot be separated from heat, snow from coldness, and the number three from oddness, so the soul cannot be separated from life. Life is essential to the soul. We say a person is dead when the soul has departed. A dead soul is a contradiction in terms. Such is the main argument in the *Phaedo* for the soul's immortality. To it the other "proofs" are subsidiary and ancillary.

This emphasis on "participation" marks a definite stage of development in the Platonic doctrine of Forms. In the dialogues the doctrine undergoes a continuous development, which for purposes of analysis may be classified according to three successive stages. The early dialogues represent the Form (or Idea) as not the changing, not the many, not the particular, not the sensible; only by implication may it be construed as the permanent, the one, the universal, the rational. In the middle dialogues Plato sets in sharp contrast the realm of permanent unchanging realities with the world of particulars, subject to becoming and decay. He asserts explicitly that the true objects of rational knowledge and the constituents of the real world are permanent, universal Forms beyond the vicissitudes of time and change. At this stage of his thought the particulars provide little in cognition beyond an exemplification of archetypes, which are Forms. The particular seen through the agency of sense proves to be an inadequate "copy" of the universal which is discerned through it. One sees, for example, a badly drawn triangle, and yet cognizes by means of the sensuous experience of this particular a triangularity which is rationally defined. Sense-experience, epistemologically speaking, is nothing more than the *occasion* of intellectual knowledge of universals through some sort of association induced by particulars.

In one especially of his later dialogues, the *Parmenides*, Plato brings under review the question of the relationship between Forms and particulars. He critically considers accounts of this in such terms as "resemblance" and "participation." And afterward, notably in the *Sophist* and the *Philebus*, he undertakes the tasks of (a) overcoming an assumed disparity between the universal and the particular, (b) uniting the one and the many in a synthesis of knowledge, and (c) merging being and permanence with becoming and change within an intelligible realm.

FULTON H. ANDERSON

UNIVERSITY OF TORONTO
December, 1950

NOTE ON THE EDITION

To facilitate reference to passages in the dialogue the pagination of Stephanus' edition of Plato (Paris, 1578) has been used in the margins of the text.

Spelling and punctuation have been revised to conform to current American usage.

PHAEDO

CHARACTERS OF THE DIALOGUE

PHAEDO	APOLLODORUS
The Narrator	CEBES
ECHECRATES	CRITO
SOCRATES	SIMMIAS

THE SERVANT OF THE ELEVEN

SCENE—*The Prison of Socrates*

CHAP. I
Steph.
p. 58

Echecrates. Were you with Socrates yourself, Phaedo, on that day when he drank the poison in the prison, or did you hear the story from someone else?

Phaedo. I was there myself, Echecrates.

Ech. Then what was it that our master said before his death, and how did he die? I should be very glad if you would tell me. None of our citizens go very much to Athens now; and no stranger has come from there for a long time who could give us any definite account of these things, except that he drank the poison and died. We could learn nothing beyond that.

Phaedo. Then have you not heard about the trial either, how that went?

Ech. Yes, we were told of that, and we were rather surprised to find that he did not die till so long after the trial. Why was that, Phaedo?

Phaedo. It was an accident, Echecrates. The stern of the ship, which the Athenians send to Delos, happened to have been crowned on the day before the trial.

Ech. And what is this ship?

Phaedo. It is the ship, as the Athenians say, in which Theseus took the seven youths and the seven maidens to Crete, and saved

1

them from death, and himself was saved. The Athenians made a vow then to Apollo, the story goes, to send a sacred mission to Delos every year, if they should be saved; and from that time to this they have always sent it to the god, every year. They have a law to keep the city pure as soon as the mission begins, and not to execute any sentence of death until the ship has returned from Delos; and sometimes, when it is detained by contrary winds, that is a long while. The sacred mission begins when the priest of Apollo crowns the stern of the ship; and, as I said, this happened to have been done on the day before the trial. That was why Socrates lay so long in prison between his trial and his death.

II   *Ech.* But tell me about his death, Phaedo. What was said and done, and which of his friends were with our master? Or would not the authorities let them be there? Did he die alone?

Phaedo. Oh, no; some of them were there, indeed several.

Ech. It would be very good of you, if you are not busy, to tell us the whole story as exactly as you can.

Phaedo. No, I have nothing to do, and I will try to relate it. Nothing is more pleasant to me than to recall Socrates to my mind, whether by speaking of him myself or by listening to others.

Ech. Indeed, Phaedo, you will have an audience like yourself. But try to tell us everything that happened as precisely as you can.

Phaedo. Well, I myself was strangely moved on that day. I did not feel that I was being present at the death of a dear friend; I did not pity him, for he seemed to me happy, Echecrates, both in his bearing and in his words, so fearlessly and nobly did he die. I could not help thinking that the gods would watch over him still on his journey to the other world, and that when he arrived there

59   it would be well with him, if it was ever well with any man. Therefore I had scarcely any feeling of pity, as you would expect at such a mournful time. Neither did I feel the pleasure which I usually felt at our philosophical discussions; for our talk was of philosophy. A very singular feeling came over me, a strange mixture of pleasure and of pain when I remembered that he was presently to die. All of us who were there were in much the same state, laughing and crying by turns; particularly Apollodorus. I think you know the man and his ways.

Ech. Of course I do.

Phaedo. Well, he did not restrain himself at all and I myself and the others were greatly agitated too.

Ech. Who were there, Phaedo?

Phaedo. Of native Athenians, there was this Apollodorus, and Critobulus, and his father Crito, and Hermogenes, and Epigenes, and Aeschines, and Antisthenes. Then there was Ctesippus the Paeanian, and Menexenus, and some other Athenians. Plato I believe was ill.

Ech. Were any strangers there?

Phaedo. Yes, there was Simmias of Thebes, and Cebes, and Phaedondes; and Eucleides and Terpsion from Megara.

Ech. But Aristippus and Cleombrotus, were they present?

Phaedo. No, they were not. They were said to be in Aegina.

Ech. Was anyone else there?

Phaedo. No, I think that these were all.

Ech. Then tell us about your conversation.

Phaedo. I will try to relate the whole story to you from the beginning. On the previous days I and the others had always met in the morning at the court where the trial was held, which was close to the prison; and then we had gone in to Socrates. We used to wait each morning until the prison was opened, conversing, for it was not opened early. When it was opened we used to go in to Socrates, and we generally spent the whole day with him. But on that morning we met earlier than usual; for the evening before we had learned, on leaving the prison, that the ship had arrived from Delos. So we arranged to be at the usual place as early as possible. When we reached the prison, the porter, who generally let us in, came out to us and bade us wait a little, and not to go in until he summoned us himself: "For the Eleven," he said, "are releasing Socrates from his fetters and giving directions for his death today." In no great while he returned and bade us enter. So we went in and found Socrates just released, and Xanthippe— you know her—sitting by him, holding his child in her arms. When Xanthippe saw us, she wailed aloud, and cried, in her woman's way, "This is the last time, Socrates, that you will talk with your friends, or they with you." And Socrates glanced at

III

60

Crito, and said, "Crito, let her be taken home." So some of Crito's servants led her away weeping bitterly and beating her breast. But Socrates sat up on the bed, and bent his leg and rubbed it with his hand, and while he was rubbing it said to us, How strange a thing is what men call pleasure! How wonderful is its relation to pain, which seems to be the opposite of it! They will not come to a man together; but if he pursues the one and gains it, he is almost forced to take the other also, as if they were two distinct things united at one end. And I think, said he, that if Aesop had noticed them he would have composed a fable about them, to the effect that God had wished to reconcile them when they were quarrelling, and that, when he could not do that, he joined their ends together; and that therefore whenever the one comes to a man, the other is sure to follow. That is just the case with me. There was pain in my leg caused by the chains, and now, it seems, pleasure is come following the pain.

IV   Cebes interrupted him and said, By the bye, Socrates, I am glad that you reminded me. Several people have been inquiring about your poems, the hymn to Apollo, and Aesop's fables which you have put into meter, and only a day or two ago Evenus asked me what was your reason for writing poetry on coming here, when you had never written a line before. So if you wish me to be able to answer him when he asks me again, as I know that he will, tell me what to say.

     Then tell him the truth, Cebes, he said. Say that it was from no wish to pose as a rival to him, or to his poems. I knew that it would not be easy to do that. I was only testing the meaning of certain dreams and acquitting my conscience about them, in case they should be bidding me make this kind of music. The fact is this. The same dream used often to come to me in my past life, appearing in different forms at different times, but always saying the same words, "Socrates, work at music and compose it." Formerly I used to think that the dream was encouraging me and

61   cheering me on in what was already the work of my life, just as the spectators cheer on different runners in a race. I supposed that the dream was encouraging me to create the music at which I was working already, for I thought that philosophy was the highest

music, and my life was spent in philosophy. But then, after the trial, when the feast of the god delayed my death, it occurred to me that the dream might possibly be bidding me create music in the popular sense, and that in that case I ought to do so, and not to disobey. I thought that it would be safer to acquit my conscience by creating poetry in obedience to the dream before I departed. So first I composed a hymn to the god whose feast it was. And then I turned such fables of Aesop as I knew, and had ready to my hand, into verse, taking those which came first; for I reflected that a man who means to be a poet has to use fiction and not facts for his poems; and I could not invent fiction myself.

Tell Evenus this, Cebes, and bid him farewell from me; and tell him to follow me as quickly as he can, if he is wise. I, it seems, shall depart today, for that is the will of the Athenians. V

And Simmias said, What strange advice to give Evenus, Socrates! I have often met him, and from what I have seen of him I think that he is certainly not at all the man to take it, if he can help it.

What, he said, is not Evenus a philosopher?

Yes, I suppose so, replied Simmias.

Then Evenus will wish to die, he said, and so will every man who is worthy of having any part in this study. But he will not lay violent hands on himself; for that, they say, is wrong. And as he spoke he put his legs off the bed on to the ground, and remained sitting thus for the rest of the conversation.

Then Cebes asked him, What do you mean, Socrates, by saying that it is wrong for a man to lay violent hands on himself, but that the philosopher will wish to follow the dying man?

What, Cebes? Have you and Simmias been with Philolaus, and not heard about these things?

Nothing very definite, Socrates.

Well, I myself only speak of them from hearsay, yet there is no reason why I should not tell you what I have heard. Indeed, as I am setting out on a journey to the other world, what could be more fitting for me than to talk about my journey and to consider what we imagine to be its nature? How could we better employ the interval between this and sunset?

VI   Then what is their reason for saying that it is wrong for a
man to kill himself, Socrates? It is quite true that I have heard
Philolaus say, when he was living at Thebes, that it is not right;
and I have heard the same thing from others, too, but I never
heard anything definite on the subject from any of them.

62   You must be of good cheer, said he, possibly you will hear
something some day. But perhaps you will be surprised if I say
that this law, unlike every other law to which mankind is subject,
is absolute and without exception; and that it is not true that death
is better than life only for some persons and at some times. And
perhaps you will be surprised if I tell you that these men, for
whom it would be better to die, may not do themselves a service,
but that they must await a benefactor from without.

Oh indeed, said Cebes, laughing quietly, and speaking in his
native dialect.

Indeed, said Socrates, so stated it may seem strange, and yet
perhaps a reason may be given for it. The reason which the
secret teaching[1] gives, that man is in a kind of prison, and that
he may not set himself free, nor escape from it, seems to me rather
profound and not easy to fathom. But I do think, Cebes, that it
is true that the gods are our guardians, and that we men are a
part of their property. Do you not think so?

I do, said Cebes.

Well then, said he, if one of your possessions were to kill
itself, though you had not signified that you wished it to die,
should you not be angry with it? Should you not punish it, if
punishment were possible?

Certainly, he replied.

Then in this way perhaps it is not unreasonable to hold that
no man has a right to take his own life, but that he must wait until
God sends some necessity upon him, as has now been sent
upon me.

VII   Yes, said Cebes, that does seem natural. But you were saying
just now that the philosopher will desire to die. Is not that a
paradox, Socrates, if what we have just been saying, that God is

[1] The Esoteric system of the Pythagoreans.

our guardian and that we are his property, be true? It is not reasonable to say that the wise man will be content to depart from this service, in which the gods, who are the best of all rulers, rule him. He will hardly think that when he becomes free he will take better care of himself than the gods take of him. A fool perhaps might think so, and say that he would do well to run away from his master; he might not consider that he ought not to run away from a good master, but that he ought to remain with him as long as possible, and so in his thoughtlessness he might run away. But the wise man will surely desire to remain always with one who is better than himself. But if this be true, Socrates, the reverse of what you said just now seems to follow. The wise man should grieve to die, and the fool should rejoice.

I thought Socrates was pleased with Cebes' insistence. He 63 looked at us, and said, Cebes is always examining arguments. He will not be convinced at once by anything that one says.

Yes, Socrates, said Simmias, but I do think that now there is something in what Cebes says. Why should really wise men want to run away from masters who are better than themselves, and lightly quit their service? And I think Cebes is aiming his argument at you, because you are so ready to leave us, and the gods, who are good rulers, as you yourself admit.

You are right, he said. I suppose you mean that I must defend myself against your charge, as if I were in a court of justice.

That is just our meaning, said Simmias.

Well then, he replied, let me try to make a more successful VIII defense to you than I did to the judges at my trial. I should be wrong, Cebes and Simmias, he went on, not to grieve at death, if I did not think that I was going to live both with other gods who are good and wise, and with men who have died and who are better than the men of this world. But you must know that I hope that I am going to live among good men, though I am not quite sure of that. But I am as sure as I can be in such matters that I am going to live with gods who are very good masters. And therefore I am not so much grieved at death; I am confident that the dead have some kind of existence, and, as has been said of old, an existence that is far better for the good than for the wicked.

Well, Socrates, said Simmias, do you mean to go away and keep this belief to yourself, or will you let us share it with you? It seems to me that we too have an interest in this good. And it will also serve as your defense, if you can convince us of what you say.

I will try, he replied. But I think Crito has been wanting to speak to me. Let us first hear what he has to say.

Only, Socrates, said Crito, that the man who is going to give you the poison has been telling me to warn you not to talk much. He says that talking heats people, and that the action of the poison must not be counteracted by heat. Those who excite themselves sometimes have to drink it two or three times.

Let him be, said Socrates; let him mind his own business, and be prepared to give me the poison twice, or, if need be, thrice.

I knew that would be your answer, said Crito, but the man has been importunate.

Never mind him, he replied. But I wish now to explain to you, my judges, why it seems to me that a man who has really spent his life in philosophy has reason to be of good cheer when 64 he is about to die, and may well hope after death to gain in the other world the greatest good. I will try to show you, Simmias and Cebes, how this may be.

IX   The world, perhaps, does not see that those who rightly engage in philosophy study only dying and death. And, if this be true, it would be surely strange for a man all through his life to desire only death, and then, when death comes to him, to be vexed at it, when it has been his study and his desire for so long.

Simmias laughed, and said: Indeed, Socrates, you make me laugh, though I am scarcely in a laughing humor now. If the multitude heard that, I fancy they would think that what you say of philosophers is quite true; and my countrymen would entirely agree with you that philosophers are indeed eager to die, and they would say that they know full well that philosophers deserve to be put to death.

And they would be right, Simmias, except in saying that

they know it. They do not know in what sense the true philosopher
is eager to die, or what kind of death he deserves, or in what sense
he deserves it. Let us dismiss them from our thoughts, and converse by ourselves. Do we believe death to be anything?

We do, replied Simmias.

And do we not believe it to be the separation of the soul
from the body? Does not death mean that the body comes to
exist by itself, separated from the soul, and that the soul exists by
herself, separated from the body? What is death but that?

It is that, he said.

Now consider, my good friend, if you and I are agreed on
another point which I think will help us to understand the question
better. Do you think that a philosopher will care very much
about what are called pleasures, such as the pleasures of eating
and drinking?

Certainly not, Socrates, said Simmias.

Or about the pleasures of sexual passion?

Indeed, no.

And, do you think that he holds the remaining cares of the
body in high esteem? Will he think much of getting fine clothes,
and sandals, and other bodily adornments, or will he despise them,
except so far as he is absolutely forced to meddle with them?

The real philosopher, I think, will despise them, he replied.

In short, said he, you think that his studies are not concerned
with the body? He stands aloof from it, as far as he can, and
turns toward the soul?

I do.

Well then, in these matters, first, it is clear that the philosopher   65
releases his soul from communion with the body, so far as he can,
beyond all other men?

It is.

And does not the world think, Simmias, that if a man has
no pleasure in such things, and does not take his share in them,
his life is not worth living? Do not they hold that he who thinks
nothing of bodily pleasures is almost as good as dead?

Indeed you are right.

X   But what about the actual acquisition of wisdom? If the body is taken as a companion in the search for wisdom, is it a hindrance or not? For example, do sight and hearing convey any real truth to men? Are not the very poets forever telling us that we neither hear nor see anything accurately? But if these senses of the body are not accurate or clear, the others will hardly be so, for they are all less perfect than these, are they not?

Yes, I think so, certainly, he said.

Then when does the soul attain truth? he asked. We see that, as often as she seeks to investigate anything in company with the body, the body leads her astray.

True.

Is it not by reasoning, if at all, that any real truth becomes manifest to her?

Yes.

And she reasons best, I suppose, when none of the senses, whether hearing, or sight, or pain, or pleasure, harasses her; when she has dismissed the body, and released herself as far as she can from all intercourse or contact with it, and so, coming to be as much alone with herself as is possible, strives after real truth.

That is so.

And here too the soul of the philosopher very greatly despises the body, and flies from it, and seeks to be alone by herself, does she not?

Clearly.

And what do you say to the next point, Simmias? Do we say that there is such a thing as absolute justice, or not?

Indeed we do.

And absolute beauty, and absolute good?

Of course.

Have you ever seen any of them with your eyes?

Indeed I have not, he replied.

Did you ever grasp them with any bodily sense? I am speaking of all absolutes, whether size, or health, or strength; in a word, of the essence or real being of everything. Is the very truth of things contemplated by the body? Is it not rather the

case that the man who prepares himself most carefully to appre-
hend by his intellect the essence of each thing which he examines
will come nearest to the knowledge of it?

Certainly.

And will not a man attain to this pure thought most completely
if he goes to each thing, as far as he can, with his mind alone,
taking neither sight nor any other sense along with his reason
in the process of thought, to be an encumbrance? In every case   66
he will pursue pure and absolute being, with his pure intellect
alone. He will be set free as far as possible from the eye and
the ear and, in short, from the whole body, because intercourse
with the body troubles the soul, and hinders her from gaining truth
and wisdom. Is it not he who will attain the knowledge of real
being, if any man will?

Your words are admirably true, Socrates, said Simmias.

And, he said, must not all this cause real philosophers to   XI
reflect, and make them say to each other, It seems that there is a
narrow path which will bring us safely to our journey's end, with
reason as our guide. As long as we have this body, and an evil
of that sort is mingled with our souls, we shall never fully gain
what we desire; and that is truth. For the body is forever taking
up our time with the care which it needs; and, besides, whenever
diseases attack it, they hinder us in our pursuit of real being.
It fills us with passions, and desires, and fears, and all manner of
phantoms, and much foolishness; and so, as the saying goes, in
very truth we can never think at all for it. It alone and its desires
cause wars and factions and battles; for the origin of all wars is
the pursuit of wealth,[2] and we are forced to pursue wealth because
we live in slavery to the cares of the body. And therefore, for
all these reasons, we have no leisure for philosophy. And last of
all, if we ever are free from the body for a time, and then turn to
examine some matter, it falls in our way at every step of the
inquiry, and causes confusion and trouble and panic, so that we
cannot see the truth for it. Verily we have learned that if we are
to have any pure knowledge at all, we must be freed from the

[2] Cf. *Republic* 373d.

body; the soul by herself must behold things as they are. Then, it seems, after we are dead, we shall gain the wisdom which we desire, and for which we say we have a passion, but not while we are alive, as the argument shows. For if it be not possible to have pure knowledge while the body is with us, one of two things must be true: either we cannot gain knowledge at all, or we can gain it only after death. For then, and not till then, will the soul exist by herself, separate from the body. And while we live, we shall come nearest to knowledge, if we have no communion or intercourse with the body beyond what is absolutely necessary, and if we are not defiled with its nature. We must live pure from it until God himself releases us. And when we are thus pure and released from its follies, we shall dwell, I suppose, with others who are pure like ourselves, and we shall of ourselves know all that is pure; and that may be the truth. For I think that the impure is not allowed to attain to the pure. Such, Simmias, I fancy must needs be the language and the reflections of the true lovers of knowledge. Do you not agree with me?

Most assuredly I do, Socrates.

And, my friend, said Socrates, if this be true, I have good hope that, when I reach the place whither I am going, I shall there, if anywhere, gain fully that which we have sought so earnestly in the past. And so I shall set forth cheerfully on the journey that is appointed me today, and so may every man who thinks that his mind is prepared and purified.

That is quite true, said Simmias.

And does not the purification consist, as we have said, in separating the soul from the body, as far as is possible, and in accustoming her to collect and rally herself together from the body on every side, and to dwell alone by herself as much as she can, both now and hereafter, released from the bondage of the body?

Yes, certainly, he said.

Is not what we call death a release and separation of the soul from the body?

Undoubtedly, he replied.

And the true philosopher, we hold, is alone in his constant

desire to set his soul free? His study is simply the release and separation of the soul from the body, is it not?

Clearly.

Would it not be absurd then, as I began by saying, for a man to complain at death coming to him, when in his life he has been preparing himself to live as nearly in a state of death as he could? Would not that be absurd?

Yes, indeed.

In truth, then, Simmias, he said, the true philosopher studies to die, and to him of all men is death least terrible. Now look at the matter in this way. In everything he is at enmity with his body, and he longs to possess his soul alone. Would it not then be most unreasonable if he were to fear and complain when he has his desire, instead of rejoicing to go to the place where he hopes to gain the wisdom that he has passionately longed for all his life, and to be released from the company of his enemy? Many a man has willingly gone to the other world, when a human love or wife or son has died, in the hope of seeing there those whom he longed for, and of being with them: and will a man who has a real passion for wisdom, and a firm hope of really finding wisdom in the other world and nowhere else, grieve at death, and not depart rejoicing? Nay, my friend, you ought not to think that, if he be truly a philosopher. He will be firmly convinced that there and nowhere else will he meet with wisdom in its purity. And if this be so, would it not, I repeat, be very unreasonable for such a man to fear death?

Yes, indeed, he replied, it would.

Does not this show clearly, he said, that any man whom you see grieving at the approach of death is after all no lover of wisdom, but a lover of his body? He is also, most likely, a lover either of wealth, or of honor, or, it may be, of both.

Yes, he said, it is as you say.

Well then, Simmias, he went on, does not what is called courage belong especially to the philosopher?

Certainly I think so, he replied.

And does not temperance, the quality which even the world

calls temperance, and which means to despise and control and govern the passions—does not temperance belong only to such men as most despise the body, and pass their lives in philosophy?

Of necessity, he replied.

For if you will consider the courage and the temperance of other men, said he, you will find that they are strange things.

How so, Socrates?

You know, he replied, that all other men regard death as one of the great evils to which mankind is subject?

Indeed they do, he said.

And when the brave men of them submit to death, do not they do so from a fear of still greater evils?

Yes.

Then all men but the philosopher are brave from fear and because they are afraid. Yet it is rather a strange thing for a man to be brave out of fear and cowardice.

Indeed it is.

And are not the orderly men of them in exactly the same case? Are not they temperate from a kind of intemperance? We should say that this cannot be; but in them this state of foolish temperance comes to that. They desire certain pleasures, and fear to lose them; and so they abstain from other pleasures because they are mastered by these. Intemperance is defined to mean being under the dominion of pleasure, yet they only master certain pleasures because they are mastered by others. But that is exactly what I said just now—that, in a way, they are made temperate from intemperance.

It seems to be so.

My dear Simmias, I fear that virtue is not really to be bought in this way, by bartering pleasure for pleasure, and pain for pain, and fear for fear, and the greater for the less, like coins. There is only one sterling coin for which all these things ought to be exchanged, and that is wisdom. All that is bought and sold for this and with this, whether courage, or temperance, or justice, is real; in one word, true virtue cannot be without wisdom, and it matters nothing whether pleasure, and fear, and all other such things are present or absent. But I think that the virtue which is

composed of pleasures and fears bartered with one another, and
severed from wisdom, is only a shadow of true virtue, and that it
has no freedom, nor health, nor truth. True virtue in reality is
a kind of purifying from all these things; and temperance, and
justice, and courage, and wisdom itself are the purification. And
I fancy that the men who established our mysteries had a very
real meaning: in truth they have been telling us in parables all
the time that whosoever comes to Hades uninitiated and profane
will lie in the mire, while he that has been purified and initiated
shall dwell with the gods. For "the thyrsus-bearers are many,"
as they say in the mysteries, "but the inspired few." And by
these last, I believe, are meant only the true philosophers. And
I in my life have striven as hard as I was able, and have left
nothing undone, that I might become one of them. Whether I
have striven in the right way, and whether I have succeeded or
not, I suppose that I shall learn in a little while, when I reach
the other world, if it be the will of God.

That is my defense, Simmias and Cebes, to show that I have
reason for not being angry or grieved at leaving you and my
masters here. I believe that in the next world, no less than in this,
I shall meet with good masters and friends, though the multitude
are incredulous of it. And if I have been more successful with
you in my defense than I was with my Athenian judges, it is well.

When Socrates had finished, Cebes replied to him, and said, XIV
I think that for the most part you are right, Socrates. But men
are very incredulous of what you have said of the soul. They 70
fear that she will no longer exist anywhere when she has left the
body, but that she will be destroyed and perish on the very day
of death. They think that the moment that she is released and
leaves the body, she will be dissolved and vanish away like breath
or smoke, and thenceforward cease to exist at all. If she were to
exist somewhere as a whole, released from the evils which you
enumerated just now, we should have good reason to hope,
Socrates, that what you say is true. But it will need no little
persuasion and assurance to show that the soul exists after death,
and continues to possess any power or wisdom.

True, Cebes, said Socrates; but what are we to do? Do you

wish to converse about these matters and see if what I say is probable?

I for one, said Cebes, should gladly hear your opinion about them.

I think, said Socrates, that no one who heard me now, even if he were a comic poet, would say that I am an idle talker about things which do not concern me. So, if you wish it, let us examine this question.

XV   Let us consider whether or not the souls of men exist in the next world after death, thus. There is an ancient belief, which we remember, that on leaving this world they exist there, and that they return hither and are born again from the dead. But if it be true that the living are born from the dead, our souls must exist in the other world; otherwise they could not be born again. It will be a sufficient proof that this is so if we can really prove that the living are born only from the dead. But if this is not so, we shall have to find some other argument.

Exactly, said Cebes.

Well, said he, the easiest way of answering the question will be to consider it not in relation to men only, but also in relation to all animals and plants, and in short to all things that are generated. Is it the case that everything which has an opposite is generated only from its opposite? By opposites I mean the honorable and the base, the just and the unjust, and so on in a thousand other instances. Let us consider then whether it is necessary for everything that has an opposite to be generated only from its own opposite. For instance, when anything becomes greater, I suppose it must first have been less and then become greater?

Yes.

71   And if a thing becomes less, it must have been greater, and afterward become less?

That is so, said he.

And further, the weaker is generated from the stronger, and the swifter from the slower?

Certainly.

And the worse is generated from the better, and the more just from the more unjust?

Of course.

Then it is sufficiently clear to us that all things are generated in this way, opposites from opposites?

Quite so.

And in every pair of opposites, are there not two generations between the two members of the pair, from the one to the other, and then back again from the other to the first? Between the greater and the less are growth and diminution, and we say that the one grows and the other diminishes, do we not?

Yes, he said.

And there is division and composition, and cold and hot, and so on. In fact, is it not a universal law, even though we do not always express it in so many words, that opposites are generated always from one another, and that there is a process of generation from one to the other?

It is, he replied.

Well, said he, is there an opposite to life, in the same way that **XVI** sleep is the opposite of being awake?

Certainly, he answered.

What is it?

Death, he replied.

Then if life and death are opposites, they are generated the one from the other: they are two, and between them there are two generations. Is it not so?

Of course.

Now, said Socrates, I will explain to you one of the two pairs of opposites of which I spoke just now, and its generations, and you shall explain to me the other. Sleep is the opposite of waking. From sleep is produced the state of waking, and from the state of waking is produced sleep. Their generations are, first, to fall asleep; secondly, to awake. Is that clear? he asked.

Yes, quite.

Now then, said he, do you tell me about life and death. Death is the opposite of life, is it not?

It is.

And they are generated the one from the other?

Yes.

Then what is that which is generated from the living?

The dead, he replied.

And what is generated from the dead?

I must admit that it is the living.

Then living things and living men are generated from the dead, Cebes?

Clearly, said he.

Then our souls exist in the other world? he said.

Apparently.

Now of these two generations the one is certain? Death I suppose is certain enough, is it not?

Yes, quite, he replied.

What then shall we do? said he. Shall we not assign an opposite generation to correspond? Or is nature imperfect here? Must we not assign some opposite generation to dying?

I think so, certainly, he said.

And what must it be?

To come to life again.

72   And if there be such a thing as a return to life, he said, it will be a generation from the dead to the living, will it not?

It will, certainly.

Then we are agreed on this point: namely, that the living are generated from the dead no less than the dead from the living. But we agreed that, if this be so, it is a sufficient proof that the souls of the dead must exist somewhere, whence they come into being again.

I think, Socrates, that that is the necessary result of our premises.

XVII   And I think, Cebes, said he, that our conclusion has not been an unfair one. For if opposites did not always correspond with opposites as they are generated, moving as it were round in a circle, and there were generation in a straight line forward from one opposite only, with no turning or return to the other, then, you know, all things would come at length to have the same form and be in the same state, and would cease to be generated at all.

What do you mean? he asked.

It is not at all hard to understand my meaning, he replied. If, for example, the one opposite, to go to sleep, existed without the corresponding opposite, to wake up, which is generated from the first, then all nature would at last make the tale of Endymion meaningless, and he would no longer be conspicuous; for everything else would be in the same state of sleep that he was in. And if all things were compounded together and never separated, the Chaos of Anaxagoras would soon be realized. Just in the same way, my dear Cebes, if all things in which there is any life were to die, and when they were dead were to remain in that form and not come to life again, would not the necessary result be that everything at last would be dead, and nothing alive? For if living things were generated from other sources than death, and were to die, the result is inevitable that all things would be consumed by death. Is it not so?

It is indeed, I think, Socrates, said Cebes; I think that what you say is perfectly true.

Yes, Cebes, he said, I think it is certainly so. We are not misled into this conclusion. The dead do come to life again, and the living are generated from them, and the souls of the dead exist; and with the souls of the good it is well, and with the souls of the evil it is evil.

And besides, Socrates, rejoined Cebes, if the doctrine which XVIII you are fond of stating, that our learning is only a process of recollection, be true, then I suppose we must have learned at some former time what we recollect now. And that would be impossible unless our souls had existed somewhere before they came into this human form. So that is another reason for 73 believing the soul immortal.

But, Cebes, interrupted Simmias, what are the proofs of that? Recall them to me; I am not very clear about them at present.

One argument, answered Cebes, and the strongest of all, is that if you question men about anything in the right way, they will answer you correctly of themselves. But they would not have been able to do that unless they had had within themselves knowledge and right reason. Again, show them such things as geometrical diagrams, and the proof of the doctrine is complete.[a]

And if that does not convince you, Simmias, said Socrates, look at the matter in another way and see if you agree then. You have doubts, I know, how what is called knowledge can be recollection.

Nay, replied Simmias, I do not doubt. But I want to recollect the argument about recollection. What Cebes undertook to explain has nearly brought your theory back to me and convinced me. But I am nonetheless ready to hear you undertake to explain it.

In this way, he returned. We are agreed, I suppose, that if a man remembers anything, he must have known it at some previous time.

Certainly, he said.

And are we agreed that when knowledge comes in the following way, it is recollection? When a man has seen or heard anything, or has perceived it by some other sense, and then knows not that thing only, but has also in his mind an impression of some other thing, of which the knowledge is quite different, are we not right in saying that he remembers the thing of which he has an impression in his mind?

What do you mean?

I mean this. The knowledge of a man is different from the knowledge of a lyre, is it not?

Certainly.

And you know that when lovers see a lyre, or a garment, or anything that their favorites are wont to use, they have this feeling. They know the lyre, and in their mind they receive the image of the youth whose the lyre was. That is recollection. For instance, someone seeing Simmias often is reminded of Cebes; and there are endless examples of the same thing.

Indeed there are, said Simmias.

[a] For an example of this see *Meno* 82a ff., where, as here, Socrates proves the doctrine of Reminiscence, and therefore the Immortality of the Soul, by putting judicious questions about geometry to a slave who was quite ignorant of geometry, and, with the help of diagrams, obtaining from him correct answers.

Is not that a kind of recollection, he said; and more especially when a man has this feeling with reference to things which the lapse of time and inattention have made him forget?

Yes, certainly, he replied.

Well, he went on, is it possible to recollect a man on seeing the picture of a horse, or the picture of a lyre? Or to recall Simmias on seeing a picture of Cebes?

Certainly.

And it is possible to recollect Simmias himself on seeing a picture of Simmias?

No doubt, he said.

Then in all these cases there is recollection caused by similar objects, and also by dissimilar objects?

74

XIX

There is.

But when a man has a recollection caused by similar objects, will he not have a further feeling and consider whether the likeness to that which he recollects is defective in any way or not?

He will, he said.

Now see if this is true, he went on. Do we not believe in the existence of equality—not the equality of pieces of wood or of stones, but something beyond that—equality in the abstract? Shall we say that there is such a thing, or not?

Yes indeed, said Simmias, most emphatically we will.

And do we know what this abstract equality is?

Certainly, he replied.

Where did we get the knowledge of it? Was it not from seeing the equal pieces of wood, and stones, and the like, which we were speaking of just now? Did we not form from them the idea of abstract equality, which is different from them? Or do you think that it is not different? Consider the question in this way. Do not equal pieces of wood and stones appear to us sometimes equal and sometimes unequal, though in fact they remain the same all the time?

Certainly they do.

But did absolute equals ever seem to you to be unequal, or abstract equality to be inequality?

No, never, Socrates.

Then equal things, he said, are not the same as abstract equality?

No, certainly not, Socrates.

Yet it was from these equal things, he said, which are different from abstract equality, that you have conceived and got your knowledge of abstract equality?

That is quite true, he replied.

And that whether it is like them or unlike them?

Certainly.

But that makes no difference, he said. As long as the sight of one thing brings another thing to your mind, there must be recollection, whether or no the two things are like.

That is so.

Well then, said he, do the equal pieces of wood, and other similar equal things, of which we have been speaking, affect us at all this way? Do they seem to us to be equal, in the way that abstract equality is equal? Do they come short of being like abstract equality, or not?

Indeed, they come very short of it, he replied.

Are we agreed about this? A man sees something and thinks to himself, "This thing that I see aims at being like some other thing, but it comes short and cannot be like that other thing; it is inferior"; must not the man who thinks that have known at some previous time that other thing, which he says that it resembles, and to which it is inferior?

He must.

Well, have we ourselves had the same sort of feeling with reference to equal things, and to abstract equality?

Yes, certainly.

75   Then we must have had knowledge of equality before we first saw equal things, and perceived that they all strive to be like equality, and all come short of it.

That is so.

And we are agreed also that we have not, nor could we have, obtained the idea of equality except from sight or touch or some other sense; the same is true of all the senses.

Yes, Socrates, for the purposes of the argument that is so.

At any rate it is by the senses that we must perceive that all sensible objects strive to resemble absolute equality, and are inferior to it. Is not that so?

Yes.

Then before we began to see, and to hear, and to use the other senses, we must have received the knowledge of the nature of abstract and real equality; otherwise we could not have compared equal sensible objects with abstract equality, and seen that the former in all cases strive to be like the latter, though they are always inferior to it?

That is the necessary consequence of what we have been saying, Socrates.

Did we not see, and hear, and possess the other senses as soon as we were born?

Yes, certainly.

And we must have received the knowledge of abstract equality before we had these senses?

Yes.

Then, it seems, we must have received that knowledge before we were born?

It does.

Now if we received this knowledge before our birth, and   XX were born with it, we knew, both before and at the moment of our birth, not only the equal, and the greater, and the less, but also everything of the same kind, did we not? Our present reasoning does not refer only to equality. It refers just as much to absolute good, and absolute beauty, and absolute justice, and absolute holiness; in short, I repeat, to everything which we mark with the name of the real, in the questions and answers of our dialectic. So we must have received our knowledge of all realities before we were born.

That is so.

And we must always be born with this knowledge, and must always retain it throughout life, if we have not each time forgotten it, after having received it. For to know means to receive and retain knowledge, and not to have lost it. Do not we mean by forgetting, the loss of knowledge, Simmias?

Yes, certainly, Socrates, he said.

But, I suppose, if it be the case that we lost at birth the knowledge which we received before we were born, and then afterward, by using our senses on the objects of sense, recovered the knowledge which we had previously possessed, then what we call learning is the recovering of knowledge which is already ours. And are we not right in calling that recollection?

Certainly.

76   For we have found it possible to perceive a thing by sight, or hearing, or any other sense, and thence to form a notion of some other thing, like or unlike, which had been forgotten, but with which this thing was associated. And therefore, I say, one of two things must be true. Either we are all born with this knowledge and retain it all our life; or, after birth, those whom we say are learning are only recollecting, and our knowledge is recollection.

Yes indeed, that is undoubtedly true, Socrates.

XXI   Then which do you choose, Simmias? Are we born with knowledge or do we recollect the things of which we have received knowledge before our birth?

I cannot say at present, Socrates.

Well, have you an opinion about this question? Can a man who knows give an account of what he knows, or not? What do you think about that?

Yes, of course he can, Socrates.

And do you think that everyone can give an account of the ideas of which we have been speaking?

I wish I did, indeed, said Simmias, but I am very much afraid that by this time tomorrow there will no longer be any man living able to do so as it should be done.

Then, Simmias, he said, you do not think that all men know these things?

Certainly not.

Then they recollect what they once learned?

Necessarily.

And when did our souls gain this knowledge? It cannot have been after we were born men.

No, certainly not.

Then it was before?

Yes.

Then, Simmias, our souls existed formerly, apart from our bodies, and possessed intelligence before they came into man's shape.[4]

Unless we receive this knowledge at the moment of birth, Socrates. That time still remains.

Well, my friend, and at what other time do we lose it? We agreed just now that we are not born with it; do we lose it at the same moment that we gain it, or can you suggest any other time?

I cannot, Socrates. I did not see that I was talking nonsense.

Then, Simmias, he said, is not this the truth? If, as we are XXII forever repeating, beauty, and good, and the other ideas[5] really exist, and if we refer all the objects of sensible perception to these ideas which were formerly ours, and which we find to be ours still, and compare sensible objects with them, then, just as they exist, our souls must have existed before ever we were born. But if they do not exist, then our reasoning will have been thrown away. Is it so? If these ideas exist, does it not at once follow that our souls must have existed before we were born, and if they do not exist, then neither did our souls?

Admirably put, Socrates, said Simmias. I think that the necessity is the same for the one as for the other. The reasoning 77 has reached a place of safety in the common proof of the existence of our souls before we were born and of the existence of the

[4] Cf. Wordsworth's famous *Ode on Intimations of Immortality*. It must be noticed that in one respect Wordsworth exactly reverses Plato's theory. With Wordsworth "Heaven lies about us in our infancy," and as we grow to manhood we gradually forget it. With Plato, we lose the knowledge which we possessed in a prior state of existence, at birth, and recover it, as we grow up.

[5] For a fuller account of the ideas, see 100b ff.

ideas of which you spoke. Nothing is so evident to me as that beauty, and good, and the other ideas which you spoke of just now have a very real existence indeed. Your proof is quite sufficient for me.

But what of Cebes? said Socrates. I must convince Cebes too.

I think that he is satisfied, said Simmias, though he is the most skeptical of men in argument. But I think that he is perfectly convinced that our souls existed before we were born.

XXIII But I do not think myself, Socrates, he continued, that you have proved that the soul will continue to exist when we are dead. The common fear which Cebes spoke of, that she may be scattered to the winds at death, and that death may be the end of her existence, still stands in the way. Assuming that the soul is generated and comes together from some other elements, and exists before she ever enters the human body, why should she not come to an end and be destroyed, after she has entered into the body, when she is released from it?

You are right, Simmias, said Cebes. I think that only half the required proof has been given. It has been shown that our souls existed before we were born; but it must also be shown that our souls will continue to exist after we are dead, no less than that they existed before we were born, if the proof is to be complete.

That has been shown already, Simmias and Cebes, said Sócrates, if you will combine this reasoning with our previous conclusion, that all life is generated from death. For if the soul exists in a previous state and if, when she comes into life and is born, she can only be born from death, and from a state of death, must she not exist after death too, since she has to be born again? So the point which you speak of has been already proved.

XXIV Still I think that you and Simmias would be glad to discuss this question further. Like children, you are afraid that the wind will really blow the soul away and disperse her when she leaves the body, especially if a man happens to die in a storm and not in a calm.

Cebes laughed and said, Try and convince us as if we were

afraid, Socrates; or rather, do not think that we are afraid ourselves. Perhaps there is a child within us who has these fears.
Let us try and persuade him not to be afraid of death, as if it
were a bugbear.

You must charm him every day, until you have charmed him
away, said Socrates.

And where shall we find a good charmer, Socrates, he asked,   78
now that you are leaving us?

Hellas is a large country, Cebes, he replied, and good men
may doubtless be found in it; and the nations of the Barbarians
are many. You must search them all through for such a charmer,
sparing neither money nor labor; for there is nothing on which
you could spend money more profitably. And you must search
for him among yourselves too, for you will hardly find a better
charmer than yourselves.

That shall be done, said Cebes. But let us return to the point
where we left off, if you will.

Yes, I will: why not?

Very good, he replied.

Well, said Socrates, must we not ask ourselves this question? XXV
What kind of thing is liable to suffer dispersion, and for what kind
of thing have we to fear dispersion? And then we must see
whether the soul belongs to that kind or not, and be confident
or afraid about our own souls accordingly.

That is true, he answered.

Now is it not the compound and composite which is naturally
liable to be dissolved in the same way in which it was compounded? And is not what is uncompounded alone not liable to
dissolution, if anything is not?

I think that that is so, said Cebes.

And what always remains in the same state and unchanging
is most likely to be uncompounded, and what is always changing
and never the same is most likely to be compounded, I suppose?

Yes, I think so.

Now let us return to what we were speaking of before in the
discussion, he said. Does the being, which in our dialectic we
define as meaning absolute existence, remain always in exactly

the same state, or does it change? Do absolute equality, absolute beauty, and every other absolute existence, admit of any change at all? Or does absolute existence in each case, being essentially uniform, remain the same and unchanging, and never in any case admit of any sort or kind of change whatsoever?

It must remain the same and unchanging, Socrates, said Cebes.

And what of the many beautiful things, such as men, and horses, and garments, and the like, and of all which bears the names of the ideas, whether equal, or beautiful, or anything else? Do they remain the same or is it exactly the opposite with them? In short, do they never remain the same at all, either in themselves or in their relations?

These things, said Cebes, never remain the same.

79   You can touch them, and see them, and perceive them with the other senses, while you can grasp the unchanging only by the reasoning of the intellect. These latter are invisible and not seen. Is it not so?

That is perfectly true, he said.

XXVI   Let us assume then, he said, if you will, that there are two kinds of existence, the one visible, the other invisible.

Yes, he said.

And the invisible is unchanging, while the visible is always changing.

Yes, he said again.

Are not we men made up of body and soul?

There is nothing else, he replied.

And which of these kinds of existence should we say that the body is most like, and most akin to?

The visible, he replied; that is quite obvious.

And the soul? Is that visible or invisible?

It is invisible to man, Socrates, he said.

But we mean by visible and invisible, visible and invisible to man; do we not?

Yes; that is what we mean.

Then what do we say of the soul? Is it visible or not visible?

It is not visible.

Then is it invisible?

Yes.

Then the soul is more like the invisible than the body; and the body is like the visible.

That is necessarily so, Socrates.

Have we not also said that, when the soul employs the body   XXVII
in any inquiry, and makes use of sight, or hearing, or any other sense—for inquiry with the body means inquiry with the senses—she is dragged away by it to the things which never remain the same, and wanders about blindly, and becomes confused and dizzy, like a drunken man, from dealing with things that are ever changing?

Certainly.

But when she investigates any question by herself, she goes away to the pure, and eternal, and immortal, and unchangeable, to which she is akin, and so she comes to be ever with it, as soon as she is by herself, and can be so; and then she rests from her wanderings and dwells with it unchangingly, for she is dealing with what is unchanging. And is not this state of the soul called wisdom?

Indeed, Socrates, you speak well and truly, he replied.

Which kind of existence do you think from our former and our present arguments that the soul is more like and more akin to?

I think, Socrates, he replied, that after this inquiry the very dullest man would agree that the soul is infinitely more like the unchangeable than the changeable.

And the body?

That is like the changeable.

Consider the matter in yet another way. When the soul XXVIII
and the body are united, nature ordains the one to be a slave   80
and to be ruled, and the other to be master and to rule. Tell me once again, which do you think is like the divine, and which is like the mortal? Do you not think that the divine naturally rules and has authority, and that the mortal naturally is ruled and is a slave?

I do.

Then which is the soul like?

That is quite plain, Socrates. The soul is like the divine, and the body is like the mortal.

Now tell me, Cebes, is the result of all that we have said

that the soul is most like the divine, and the immortal, and the intelligible, and the uniform, and the indissoluble, and the unchangeable; while the body is most like the human, and the mortal, and the unintelligible, and the multiform, and the dissoluble, and the changeable?   Have we any other argument to show that this is not so, my dear Cebes?

We have not.

XXIX   Then if this is so, is it not the nature of the body to be dissolved quickly, and of the soul to be wholly or very nearly indissoluble?[6]

Cretainly

You observe, he said, that after a man is dead, the visible part of him, his body, which lies in the visible world and which we call the corpse, which is subject to dissolution and decomposition, is not dissolved and decomposed at once?   It remains as it was for a considerable time, and even for a long time, if a man dies with his body in good condition and in the vigor of life. And when the body falls in and is embalmed, like the mummies of Egypt, it remains nearly entire for an immense time.   And should it decay, yet some parts of it, such as the bones and muscles, may almost be said to be immortal.   Is it not so?

Yes.

And shall we believe that the soul, which is invisible, and which goes hence to a place that is like herself, glorious, and pure, and invisible, to Hades, which is rightly called the unseen world, to dwell with the good and wise God, whither, if it be the will of God, my soul too must shortly go—shall we believe that the soul, whose nature is so glorious, and pure, and invisible, is blown away by the winds and perishes as soon as she leaves the body, as the world says?   Nay, dear Cebes and Simmias, it is not so.   I will tell you what happens to a soul which is pure at her departure, and which in her life has had no intercourse that she

---

[6] Compare Bishop Butler's *Analogy*, Pt. I, Ch. I, where a similar argument is used: the soul being indiscerptible is immortal.   The argument based on the "divine" nature of the soul is, of course, also a modern one. See *e.g.* Lord Tennyson, *In Memoriam*, LIV-LVI.

could avoid with the body, and so draws after her, when she dies, no taint of the body, but has shunned it, and gathered herself into herself, for such has been her constant study—and that only means that she has loved wisdom rightly, and has truly practiced 81 how to die. Is not this the practice of death?

Yes, certainly.

Does not the soul, then, which is in that state, go away to the invisible that is like herself, and to the divine, and the immortal, and the wise, where she is released from error, and folly, and fear, and fierce passions, and all the other evils that fall to the lot of men, and is happy, and for the rest of time lives in very truth with the gods, as they say that the initiated do? Shall we affirm this, Cebes?

Yes, certainly, said Cebes.

But if she be defiled and impure when she leaves the body, XXX from being ever with it, and serving it and loving it, and from being besotted by it and by its desires and pleasures, so that she thinks nothing true but what is bodily and can be touched, and seen, and eaten, and drunk, and used for men's lusts; if she has learned to hate, and tremble at, and fly from what is dark and invisible to the eye, and intelligible and apprehended by philosophy —do you think that a soul which is in that state will be pure and without alloy at her departure?

No, indeed, he replied.

She is penetrated, I suppose, by the corporeal, which the unceasing intercourse and company and care of the body has made a part of her nature.

Yes.

And, my dear friend, the corporeal must be burdensome, and heavy, and earthy, and visible; and it is by this that such a soul is weighed down and dragged back to the visible world, because she is afraid of the invisible world of Hades, and haunts, it is said, the graves and tombs, where shadowy forms of souls have been seen, which are the phantoms of souls which were impure at their release and still cling to the visible; which is the reason why they are seen.[7]

---

[7] Professor Jowett compares Milton, *Comus*, 463 ff.

That is likely enough, Socrates.

That is likely, certainly, Cebes; and these are not the souls of the good, but of the evil, which are compelled to wander in such places as a punishment for the wicked lives that they have lived; and their wanderings continue until, from the desire for the corporeal that clings to them, they are again imprisoned in a body.

XXXI And, he continued, they are imprisoned, probably, in the bodies of animals with habits similar to the habits which were theirs in their lifetime.

What do you mean by that, Socrates?

I mean that men who have practiced unbridled gluttony, and wantonness, and drunkenness probably enter the bodies of asses and suchlike animals. Do you not think so?

82 Certainly that is very likely.

And those who have chosen injustice, and tyranny, and robbery enter the bodies of wolves, and hawks, and kites. Where else should we say that such souls go?

No doubt, said Cebes, they go into such animals.

In short, it is quite plain, he said, whither each soul goes; each enters an animal with habits like its own.

Certainly, he replied, that is so.

And of these, he said, the happiest, who go to the best place, are those who have practiced the popular and social virtues which are called temperance and justice, and which come from habit and practice, without philosophy or reason.

And why are they the happiest?

Because it is probable that they return into a mild and social nature like their own, such as that of bees, or wasps, or ants; or, it may be, into the bodies of men, and that from them are made worthy citizens.

Very likely.

XXXII But none but the philosopher or the lover of knowledge, who is wholly pure when he goes hence, is permitted to go to the race of the gods; and therefore, my friends, Simmias and Cebes, the true philosopher is temperate and refrains from all the pleasures of the body, and does not give himself up to them. It is not squandering his substance and poverty that he fears, as the multitude and the lovers of wealth do; nor again does he dread the dishonor and disgrace of wickedness, like the lovers of power and honor. It is not for these reasons that he is temperate.

No, it would be unseemly in him if he were, Socrates, said Cebes.

Indeed it would, he replied, and therefore all those who have any care for their souls, and who do not spend their lives in forming and molding their bodies, bid farewell to such persons, and do not walk in their ways, thinking that they know not whither they are going. They themselves turn and follow whithersoever philosophy leads them, for they believe that they ought not to resist philosophy, or its deliverance and purification.

How, Socrates?

I will tell you, he replied. The lovers of knowledge know XXXIII that when philosophy receives the soul, she is fast bound in the body, and fastened to it; she is unable to contemplate what is, by herself, or except through the bars of her prison house, the body; and she is wallowing in utter ignorance. And philosophy sees that the dreadful thing about the imprisonment is that it is caused by lust, and that the captive herself is an accomplice 83 in her own captivity. The lovers of knowledge, I repeat, know that philosophy takes the soul when she is in this condition, and gently encourages her, and strives to release her from her captivity, showing her that the perceptions of the eye, and the ear, and the other senses are full of deceit, and persuading her to stand aloof from the senses and to use them only when she must, and exhorting her to rally and gather herself together, and to trust only to herself and to the real existence which she of her own self apprehends, and to believe that nothing which is subject to change, and which she perceives by other faculties, has any truth, for such things are visible and sensible, while what she herself sees is apprehended by reason and invisible. The soul of the true philosopher thinks that it would be wrong to resist this deliverance from captivity, and therefore she holds aloof, so far as she can, from pleasure, and desire, and pain, and fear; for she reckons that when a man has vehement pleasure, or fear, or pain, or desire, he suffers from them not merely the evils which might be expected, such as sickness or some loss arising from the indulgence of his desires; he suffers what is the greatest and last of evils, and does not take it into account.

What do you mean, Socrates? asked Cebes.

I mean that when the soul of any man feels vehement pleasure or pain, she is forced at the same time to think that the object, whatever it be, of these sensations is the most distinct and truest, when it is not. Such objects are chiefly visible ones, are they not?

They are.

And is it not in this state that the soul is most completely in bondage to the body?

How so?

Because every pleasure and pain has a kind of nail, and nails and pins her to the body, and gives her a bodily nature, making her think that whatever the body says is true. And so, from having the same fancies and the same pleasures as the body, she is obliged, I suppose, to come to have the same ways, and way of life: she must always be defiled with the body when she leaves it, and cannot be pure when she reaches the other world; and so she soon falls back into another body and takes root in it, like seed that is sown. Therefore she loses all part in intercourse with the divine, and pure, and uniform.

That is very true, Socrates, said Cebes.

XXXIV   It is for these reasons then, Cebes, that the real lovers of knowledge are temperate and brave; and not for the world's
84   reasons. Or do you think so?

No, certainly I do not.

Assuredly not.[8] The soul of a philosopher will consider that it is the office of philosophy to set her free. She will know that she must not give herself up once more to the bondage of pleasure and pain, from which philosophy is releasing her, and, like Penelope, do a work, only to undo it continually, weaving instead of unweaving her web. She gains for herself peace from these things, and follows reason and ever abides in it, contemplating what is true and divine and real, and fostered up by them. So

---

[8] Reading, οὐ γὰρ· ἀλλ’, with Stallbaum.

she thinks that she should live in this life, and when she dies she
believes that she will go to what is akin to and like herself, and
be released from human ills. A soul, Simmias and Cebes, that has
been so nurtured and so trained will never fear lest she should
be torn in pieces at her departure from the body, and blown away
by the winds, and vanish, and utterly cease to exist.

At these words there was a long silence. Socrates himself XXXV
seemed to be absorbed in his argument, and so were most of us.
Cebes and Simmias conversed for a little by themselves. When
Socrates observed them, he said: What? Do you think that our
reasoning is incomplete? It still offers many points of doubt and
attack, if it is to be examined thoroughly. If you are discussing
another question, I have nothing to say. But if you have any
difficulty about this one, do not hesitate to tell me what it is, and,
if you are of the opinion that the argument should be stated in a
better way, explain your views yourselves, and take me along
with you if you think that you will be more successful in my
company.

Simmias replied: Well, Socrates, I will tell you the truth.
Each of us has a difficulty, and each has been pushing on the
other and urging him to ask you about it. We were anxious
to hear what you have to say; but we were reluctant to trouble
you, for we were afraid that it might be unpleasant to you to
be asked questions now.

Socrates smiled at this answer and said, Dear me! Simmias;
I shall find it hard to convince other people that I do not consider
my fate a misfortune when I cannot convince even you of it,
and you are afraid that I am more peevish now than I used to
be. You seem to think me inferior in prophetic power to the
swans, which, when they find that they have to die, sing more
loudly than they ever sang before, for joy that they are about   85
to depart into the presence of God, whose servants they are. The
fear which men have of death themselves makes them speak falsely
of the swans, and they say that the swan is wailing at its death,
and that it sings loud for grief. They forget that no bird sings
when it is hungry, or cold, or in any pain; not even the night-
ingale, nor the swallow, nor the hoopoe, which, they assert, wail

and sing for grief. But I think that neither these birds nor the swan sing for grief. I believe that they have a prophetic power and foreknowledge of the good things in the next world, for they are Apollo's birds; and so they sing and rejoice on the day of their death, more than in all their life. And I believe that I myself am a fellow slave with the swans, and consecrated to the service of the same God, and that I have prophetic power from my master no less than they, and that I am not more despondent than they are at leaving this life. So, as far as vexing me goes, you may talk to me and ask questions as you please, as long as the Eleven of the Athenians[9] will let you.

Good, said Simmias; I will tell you my difficulty, and Cebes will tell you why he is dissatisfied with your statement. I think, Socrates, and I daresay you think so too, that it is very difficult, and perhaps impossible, to obtain clear knowledge about these matters in this life. Yet I should hold him to be a very poor creature who did not test what is said about them in every way, and persevere until he had examined the question from every side, and could do no more. It is our duty to do one of two things. We must learn, or we must discover for ourselves, the truth of these matters; or, if that be impossible, we must take the best and most irrefragable of human doctrines and, embarking on that, as on a raft, risk the voyage of life,[10] unless a stronger vessel, some divine word, could be found, on which we might take our journey more safely and more securely. And now, after what you have said, I shall not be ashamed to put a question to you; and then I shall not have to blame myself hereafter for not having said now what I think. Cebes and I have been considering your argument, and we think that it is hardly sufficient.

XXXVI   I daresay you are right, my friend, said Socrates. But tell me, where is it insufficient?

To me it is insufficient, he replied, because the very same argument might be used of a harmony, and a lyre, and its strings. It might be said that the harmony in a tuned lyre is

---

[9] Officials whose duty it was to superintend executions. Cf. 59e.

[10] See Bishop Butler's *Analogy*, Introduction.

something unseen, and incorporeal, and perfectly beautiful, and divine, while the lyre and its strings are corporeal, and with the   86 nature of bodies, and compounded, and earthly, and akin to the mortal. Now suppose that, when the lyre is broken and the strings are cut or snapped, a man were to press the same argument that you have used, and were to say that the harmony cannot have perished and that it must still exist, for it cannot possibly be that the lyre and the strings, with their mortal nature, continue to exist, though those strings have been broken, while the harmony, which is of the same nature as the divine and the immortal, and akin to them, has perished, and perished before the mortal lyre. He would say that the harmony itself must still exist somewhere, and that the wood and the strings will rot away before anything happens to it. And I think, Socrates, that you too must be aware that many of us believe the soul to be most probably a mixture and harmony of the elements by which our body is, as it were, strung and held together, such as heat and cold, and dry and wet, and the like, when they are mixed together well and in due proportion. Now if the soul is a harmony, it is clear that, when the body is relaxed out of proportion, or overstrung by disease or other evils, the soul, though most divine, must perish at once, like other harmonies of sound and of all works of art, while what remains of each body must remain for a long time, until it be burned or rotted away. What then shall we say to a man who asserts that the soul, being a mixture of the elements of the body, perishes first at what is called death?

Socrates looked keenly at us, as he often used to do, and XXXVII smiled. Simmias' objection is a fair one, he said. If any of you is readier than I am, why does he not answer? For Simmias looks like a formidable assailant. But before we answer him, I think that we had better hear what fault Cebes has to find with my reasoning, and so gain time to consider our reply. And then, when we have heard them both, we must either give in to them, if they seem to harmonize, or, if they do not, we must proceed to argue in defense of our reasoning. Come, Cebes, what is it that troubles you and makes you doubt?

I will tell you, replied Cebes. I think that the argument is

87   just where it was, and still open to our former objection. You
have shown very cleverly and, if it is not arrogant to say so,
quite conclusively that our souls existed before they entered the
human form. I don't retract my admission on that point. But I
am not convinced that they will continue to exist after we are dead.
I do not agree with Simmias' objection, that the soul is not stronger
and more lasting than the body: I think that it is very much
superior in those respects. "Well, then," the argument might reply,
"do you still doubt, when you see that the weaker part of a man
continues to exist after his death? Do you not think that the more
lasting part of him must necessarily be preserved for as long?"
See, therefore, if there is anything in what I say; for I think that
I, like Simmias, shall best express my meaning in a figure. It
seems to me that a man might use an argument similar to yours
to prove that a weaver, who had died in old age, had not in
fact perished, but was still alive somewhere, on the ground that
the garment which the weaver had woven for himself and used
to wear had not perished or been destroyed. And if anyone
were incredulous, he might ask whether a human being, or a
garment constantly in use and wear, lasts the longest; and on
being told that a human being lasts much the longest, he might
think that he had shown beyond all doubt that the man was safe,
because what lasts a shorter time than the man had not perished.
But that, I suppose, is not so, Simmias; for you too must examine
what I say. Everyone would understand that such an argument
was simple nonsense. This weaver wove himself many such
garments and wore them out; he outlived them all but the last,
but he perished before that one. Yet a man is in no wise inferior
to his cloak, or weaker than it, on that account. And I think that
the soul's relation to the body may be expressed in a similar
figure. Why should not a man very reasonably say in just the
same way that the soul lasts a long time, while the body is weaker
and lasts a shorter time? But, he might go on, each soul wears
out many bodies, especially if she lives for many years. For if
the body is in a state of flux and decay in the man's lifetime,
and the soul is ever repairing the worn-out part, it will surely follow
that the soul, on perishing, will be clothed in her last robe, and

perish before that alone. But when the soul has perished, then the body will show its weakness and quickly rot away. So as yet we have no right to be confident, on the strength of this argument, that our souls continue to exist after we are dead. And a man might concede even more than this to an opponent who used your argument;[11] he might admit not only that our souls existed in the period before we were born, but also that there is no reason why some of them should not continue to exist in the future, and often come into being, and die again, after we are dead; for the soul is strong enough by nature to endure coming into being many times. He might grant that, without conceding that she suffers no harm in all these births, or that she is not at last wholly destroyed at one of the deaths; and he might say that no man knows when this death and dissolution of the body, which brings destruction to the soul, will be, for it is impossible for any man to find out that. But if this is true, a man's confidence about death must be an irrational confidence, unless he can prove that the soul is wholly indestructible and immortal. Otherwise everyone who is dying must fear that his soul will perish utterly this time in her separation from the body.

It made us all very uncomfortable to listen to them, as we afterward said to each other. We had been fully convinced by the previous argument; and now they seemed to overturn our conviction, and to make us distrust all the arguments that were to come, as well as the preceding ones, and to doubt if our judgment was worth anything, or even if certainty could be attained at all.

Ech. By the gods, Phaedo, I can understand your feelings very well. I myself felt inclined while you were speaking to ask myself, "Then what reasoning are we to believe in future? That of Socrates was quite convincing, and now it has fallen into discredit." For the doctrine that our soul is a harmony has always taken a wonderful hold of me, and your mentioning it reminded me that I myself had held it. And now I must begin again and find some other reasoning which shall convince me that a man's

88

XXXVIII

---

[11] Reading τῷ λέγοντι ἃ συλέγεις (Schanz).

soul does not die with him at his death. So tell me, I pray you, how did Socrates pursue the argument? Did he show any signs of uneasiness, as you say that you did, or did he come to the defense of his argument calmly? And did he defend it satisfactorily or not? Tell me the whole story as exactly as you can.

89 *Phaedo.* I have often, Echecrates, wondered at Socrates; but I never admired him more than I admired him then. There was nothing very strange in his having an answer. What I chiefly wondered at was, first, the kindness and good nature and respect with which he listened to the young men's objections; and, secondly, the quickness with which he perceived their effect upon us; and, lastly, how well he healed our wounds, and rallied us as if we were beaten and flying troops, and encouraged us to follow him, and to examine the reasoning with him.

Ech. How?

Phaedo. I will tell you. I was sitting by the bed on a stool at his right hand, and his seat was a good deal higher than mine. He stroked my head and gathered up the hair on my neck in his hand—you know he used often to play with my hair—and said, Tomorrow, Phaedo, I daresay you will cut off these beautiful locks.

I suppose so, Socrates, I replied.

You will not, if you take my advice.

Why not? I asked.

You and I will cut off our hair today, he said, if our argument be dead indeed, and we cannot bring it to life again. And I, if I were you, and the argument were to escape me, would swear an oath, as the Argives did, not to wear my hair long again until I had renewed the fight and conquered the argument of Simmias and Cebes.

But Heracles himself, they say, is not a match for two, I replied.

Then summon me to aid you, as your Iolaus, while there is still light.

Then I summon you, not as Heracles summoned Iolaus, but as Iolaus might summon Heracles.

XXXIX It will be the same, he replied. But first let us take care not to make a mistake.

What mistake? I asked.

The mistake of becoming misologists, or haters of reasoning, as men become misanthropists, he replied; for to hate reasoning is the greatest evil that can happen to us. Misology and misanthropy both come from similar causes. The latter arises out of the implicit and irrational confidence which is placed in a man who is believed by his friend to be thoroughly true and sincere and trustworthy, and who is soon afterward discovered to be a bad man and untrustworthy. This happens again and again; and when a man has had this experience many times, particularly at the hands of those whom he has believed to be his nearest and dearest friends, and he has quarrelled with many of them, he ends by hating all men and thinking that there is no good at all in anyone. Have you not seen this happen?

Yes, certainly, said I.

Is it not discreditable? he said. Is it not clear that such a man tries to deal with men without understanding human nature? Had he understood it he would have known that, in fact, good men and bad men are very few indeed, and that the majority of 90 men are neither one nor the other.

What do you mean? I asked.

Just what is true of extremely large and extremely small things, he replied. What is rarer than to find a man, or a dog, or anything else which is either extremely large or extremely small? Or again, what is rarer than to find a man who is extremely swift or slow, or extremely base or honorable, or extremely black or white? Have you not noticed that in all these cases the extremes are rare and few, and that the average specimens are abundant and many?

Yes, certainly, I replied.

And in the same way, if there were a competition in wickedness, he said, don't you think that the leading sinners would be found to be very few?

That is likely enough, said I.

Yes, it is, he replied. But this is not the point in which arguments are like men; it was you who led me on to discuss this point. The analogy is this. When a man believes some reasoning to be true, though he does not understand the art of reasoning, and then soon afterward, rightly or wrongly, comes to think that it is false, and this happens to him time after time, he ends by disbelieving in reasoning altogether. You know that persons who spend their time in disputation, come at last to think themselves the wisest of men, and to imagine that they alone have discovered that there is no soundness or certainty anywhere, either in reasoning or in things, and that all existence is in a state of perpetual flux, like the currents of the Euripus, and never remains still for a moment.

Yes, I replied, that is certainly true.

And, Phaedo, he said, if there be a system of reasoning which is true, and certain, and which our minds can grasp, it would be very lamentable that a man who has met with some of these arguments which at one time seem true and at another false should at last, in the bitterness of his heart, gladly put all the blame on the reasoning, instead of on himself and his own unskillfulness, and spend the rest of his life in hating and reviling reasoning, and lose the truth and knowledge of reality.

Indeed, I replied, that would be very lamentable.

XL First then, he said, let us be careful not to admit into our souls the notion that all reasoning is very likely unsound; let us rather think that we ourselves are not yet sound. And we must strive earnestly like men to become sound, you, my friends, for the sake of all your future life, and I, because of my death. For

91 I am afraid that at present I can hardly look at death like a philosopher; I am in a contentious mood, like the uneducated persons who never give a thought to the truth of the question about which they are disputing, but are only anxious to persuade their audience that they themselves are right. And I think that today I shall differ from them only in one thing. I shall not be anxious to persuade my audience that I am right, except by the way; but I shall be very anxious indeed to persuade myself. For see, my dear friend, how selfish my reasoning is. If what I say is true, it is well to believe it. But if there is nothing after death, at any rate I shall pain my friends less by my lamentations in the interval before I die. And this ignorance

will not last forever—that would have been an evil—it will soon
come to an end. So prepared, Simmias and Cebes, he said, I
come to the argument. And you, if you take my advice, will
think not of Socrates, but of the truth; and you will agree with
me if you think that what I say is true; otherwise you will oppose
me with every argument that you have; and be careful that, in
my anxiety to convince you, I do not deceive both you and myself,
and go away, leaving my sting behind me, like a bee.

Now let us proceed, he said. And first, if you find I have   XLI
forgotten your arguments, repeat them. Simmias, I think, has
fears and misgivings that the soul, being of the nature of a
harmony, may perish before the body, though she is more divine
and nobler than the body. Cebes, if I am not mistaken, conceded
that the soul is more enduring than the body; but he said that
no one could tell whether the soul, after wearing out many bodies
many times, did not herself perish on leaving her last body, and
whether death be not precisely this—the destruction of the soul;
for the destruction of the body is unceasing. Is there anything
else, Simmias and Cebes, which we have to examine?

They both agreed that these were the questions.

Do you reject all our previous conclusions, he asked, or only
some of them?

Only some of them, they replied.

Well, said he, what do you say of our doctrine that knowledge
is recollection, and that therefore our souls must necessarily have
existed somewhere else, before they were imprisoned in our bodies?   92

I, replied Cebes, was convinced by it at the time in a
wonderful way; and now there is no doctrine to which I adhere
more firmly.

And I am of that mind too, said Simmias; and I shall be very
much surprised if I ever change it.

But, my Theban friend, you will have to change it, said
Socrates, if this opinion of yours, that a harmony is a composite
thing, and that the soul is a harmony composed of the elements
of the body at the right tension, is to stand. You will hardly
allow yourself to assert that the harmony was in existence before
the things from which it was to be composed? Will you do that?

Certainly not, Socrates.

But you see that that is what your assertion comes to when you say that the soul existed before she came into the form and body of man, and yet that she is composed of elements which did not yet exist? Your harmony is not like what you compare it to: the lyre and the strings and the sounds, as yet untuned, come into existence first; and the harmony is composed last of all, and perishes first. How will this belief of yours accord with the other?

It will not, replied Simmias.

And yet, said he, an argument about harmony is hardly the place for a discord.

No, indeed, said Simmias.

Well, there is a discord in your argument, he said. You must choose which doctrine you will retain—that knowledge is recollection or that the soul is a harmony.

The former, Socrates, certainly, he replied. The latter has never been demonstrated to me; it rests only on probable and plausible grounds, which make it a popular opinion. I know that doctrines which ground their proofs on probabilities are impostors and that they are very apt to mislead, both in geometry and everything else, if one is not on one's guard against them. But the doctrine about recollection and knowledge rests upon a foundation which claims belief. We agreed that the soul exists before she ever enters the body, as surely as the essence itself which has the name of real being exists.[12] And I am persuaded that I believe in this essence rightly and on sufficient evidence. It follows therefore, I suppose, that I cannot allow myself or anyone else to say that the soul is a harmony.

And, consider the question in another way, Simmias, said
93 Socrates. Do you think that a harmony or any other composition can exist in a state other than the state of the elements of which it is composed?

Certainly not.

Nor, I suppose, can it do or suffer anything beyond what they do and suffer?

[12] Reading **οὐτὴ αὐτῆς** (Schanz).

He assented.

A harmony therefore cannot lead the elements of which it is composed; it must follow them?

He agreed.

And much less can it be moved, or make a sound, or do anything else in opposition to its parts.

Much less, indeed, he replied.

Well, is not every harmony by nature a harmony according as it is adjusted?

I don't understand you, he replied.

If it is tuned more, and to a greater extent, he said, supposing that to be possible, will it not be more a harmony, and to a greater extent, while if it is tuned less, and to a smaller extent, will it not be less a harmony, and to a smaller extent?

Certainly.

Well, is this true of the soul? Can one soul be more a soul, and to a greater extent, or less a soul, and to a smaller extent, than another, even in the smallest degree?

Certainly not, he replied.

Well then, he replied, please tell me this; is not one soul said to have intelligence and virtue and to be good, while another is said to have folly and vice and to be bad? And is it not true?

Yes, certainly.

What then will those who assert that the soul is a harmony say that the virtue and the vice which are in our souls are? Another harmony and another discord? Will they say that the good soul is in tune, and that, herself a harmony, she has within herself another harmony, and that the bad soul is out of tune herself, and has no other harmony within her?

I, said Simmias, cannot tell. But it is clear that they would have to say something of the kind.

But it has been conceded, he said, that one soul is never more or less a soul than another. In other words, we have agreed that one harmony is never more, or to a greater extent, or less, or to a smaller extent a harmony than another. Is it not so?

Yes, certainly.

And the harmony which is neither more nor less a harmony, is not more or less tuned. Is that so?

Yes.

And has that which is neither more nor less tuned a greater, or a less, or an equal share of harmony?

An equal share.

Then, since one soul is never more nor less a soul than another, it has not been more or less tuned either?

True.

Therefore it can have no greater share of harmony or of discord?

Certainly not.

And, therefore, can one soul contain more vice or virtue than another, if vice be discord and virtue harmony?

By no means.

94   Or rather, Simmias, to speak quite accurately, I suppose that there will be no vice in any soul if the soul is a harmony. I take it there can never be any discord in a harmony which is a perfect harmony.

Certainly not.

Neither can a soul, if it be a perfect soul, have any vice in it?

No; that follows necessarily from what has been said.

Then the result of this reasoning is that all the souls of all living creatures will be equally good if the nature of all souls is to be equally souls.

Yes, I think so, Socrates, he said.

And do you think that this is true, he asked, and that this would have been the fate of our argument, if the hypothesis that the soul is a harmony had been correct?

No, certainly not, he replied.

XLII   Well, said he, of all the parts of a man, should you not say that it was the soul, and particularly the wise soul, which rules?

I should.

Does she yield to the passions of the body or does she oppose them? I mean this. When the body is hot and thirsty, does not the soul drag it away and prevent it from drinking, and when it is hungry does she not prevent it from eating? And do we not see her opposing the passions of the body in a thousand other ways?

Yes, certainly.

But we have also agreed that, if she is a harmony, she can never give a sound contrary to the tensions, and relaxations, and vibrations, and other changes of the elements of which she is composed; that she must follow them, and can never lead them?

Yes, he replied, we certainly have.

Well, now, do we not find the soul acting in just the opposite way, and leading all the elements of which she is said to consist, and opposing them in almost everything all through life; and lording it over them in every way, and chastising them, sometimes severely, and with a painful discipline, such as gymnastic and medicine, and sometimes lightly; sometimes threatening and sometimes admonishing the desires and passions and fears, as though she were speaking to something other than herself, as Homer makes Odysseus do in the *Odyssey*, where he says that

> He smote upon his breast, and chid his heart:
> "Endure, my heart, e'en worse hast thou endured."[13]

Do you think that when Homer wrote that, he supposed the soul to be a harmony and capable of being led by the passions of the body, and not of a nature to lead them and be their lord, being herself far too divine a thing to be like a harmony?

Certainly, Socrates, I think not.

Then, my excellent friend, it is quite wrong to say that the soul is a harmony. For then, you see, we should not be in agreement either with the divine poet Homer or with ourselves. 95

That is true, he replied.

Very good, said Socrates; I think that we have contrived to XLIV
appease our Theban Harmonia with tolerable success. But how about Cadmus, Cebes? he said. How shall we appease him, and with what reasoning?

I daresay that you will find out how to do it, said Cebes. At

[13] Homer *Odyssey* XX. 17.

all events you have argued that the soul is not a harmony in a way which surprised me very much. When Simmias was stating his objection, I wondered how anyone could possibly dispose of his argument; and so I was very much surprised to see it fall before the very first onset of yours. I should not wonder if the same fate awaited the argument of Cadmus.

My good friend, said Socrates, do not be overconfident, or some evil eye will overturn the argument that is to come. However, that we will leave to God; let us, like Homer's heroes, "advancing boldly," see if there is anything in what you say. The sum of what you seek is this. You require me to prove to you that the soul is indestructible and immortal; for if it be not so, you think that the confidence of a philosopher, who is confident in death, and who believes that when he is dead he will fare infinitely better in the other world than if he had lived a different sort of life in this world, is a foolish and idle confidence. You say that to show that the soul is strong and godlike, and that she existed before we were born men, is not enough; for that does not necessarily prove her immortality, but only that she lasts a long time, and has existed an enormous while, and has known and done many things in a previous state. Yet she is not any the more immortal for that; her very entrance into man's body was, like a disease, the beginning of her destruction. And, you say, she passes this life in misery, and at last perishes in what we call death. You think that it makes no difference at all to the fears of each one of us, whether she enters the body once or many times; for everyone but a fool must fear death, if he does not know and cannot prove that she is immortal. That, I think, Cebes, is the substance of your objection. I state it again and again on purpose, that nothing may escape us, and that you may add to it or take away from it anything that you wish.

Cebes replied: No, that is my meaning. I don't want to add or to take away anything at present.

XLV   Socrates paused for some time and thought. Then he said, It is not an easy question that you are raising, Cebes. We must examine fully the whole subject of the causes of generation and
96   decay. If you like, I will give you my own experiences, and if

you think that you can make use of anything that I say, you may employ it to satisfy your misgivings.

Indeed, said Cebes, I should like to hear your experiences.

Listen, then, and I will tell you, Cebes, he replied. When I was a young man, I had a passionate desire for the wisdom which is called Physical Science. I thought it a splendid thing to know the causes of everything; why a thing comes into being, and why it perishes, and why it exists. I was always worrying myself with such questions as, Do living creatures take a definite form, as some persons say, from the fermentation of heat and cold? Is it the blood, or the air, or fire by which we think? Or is it none of these, but the brain which gives the senses of hearing and sight and smell, and do memory and opinion come from these, and knowledge from memory and opinion when in a state of quiescence? Again, I used to examine the destruction of these things, and the changes of the heaven and the earth, until at last I concluded that I was wholly and absolutely unfitted for these studies. I will prove that to you conclusively. I was so completely blinded by these studies that I forgot what I had formerly seemed to myself and to others to know quite well; I unlearned all that I had been used to think that I understood; even the cause of man's growth. Formerly I had thought it evident on the face of it that the cause of growth was eating and drinking, and that, when from food flesh is added to flesh, and bone to bone, and in the same way to the other parts of the body their proper elements, then by degrees the small bulk grows to be large, and so the boy becomes a man. Don't you think that my belief was reasonable?

I do, said Cebes.

Then here is another experience for you. I used to feel no doubt, when I saw a tall man standing by a short one, that the tall man was, it might be, a head the taller, or, in the same way, that one horse was bigger than another. I was even clearer that ten was more than eight by the addition of two, and that a thing two cubits long was longer by half its length than a thing one cubit long.

And what do you think now? asked Cebes.

I think that I am very far from believing that I know the

cause of any of these things. Why, when you add one to one, I am not sure either that the one to which one is added has become two, or that the one added and the one to which it is added become, by the addition, two. I cannot understand how, when they are brought together, this union, or placing of one by the other, should be the cause of their becoming two, whereas, when they were separated, each of them was one, and they were not two. Nor, again, if you divide one into two, can I convince myself that this division is the cause of one becoming two; for then a thing becomes two from exactly the opposite cause. In the former case it was because two units were brought together, and the one was added to the other; while now it is because they are separated, and the one divided from the other. Nor, again, can I persuade myself that I know how one is generated; in short, this method does not show me the cause of the generation or destruction or existence of anything. I have in my own mind a confused idea of another method, but I cannot admit this one for a moment.

XLVI But one day I listened to a man who said that he was reading from a book of Anaxagoras, which affirmed that it is Mind which orders and is the cause of all things. I was delighted with this theory; it seemed to me to be right that Mind should be the cause of all things, and I thought to myself, If this is so, then Mind will order and arrange each thing in the best possible way. So if we wish to discover the cause of the generation or destruction or existence of a thing, we must discover how it is best for that thing to exist, or to act, or to be acted on. Man therefore has only to consider what is best and fittest for himself, or for other things, and then it follows necessarily that he will know what is bad; for both are included in the same science. These reflections made me very happy: I thought that I had found in Anaxagoras a teacher of the cause of existence after my own heart, and I expected that he would tell me first whether the earth is flat or round, and that he would then go on to explain to me the cause and the necessity, and tell me what is best, and that it is best for the earth to be of that shape. If he said that the earth was in the center of the universe, I thought that he would explain that it was best for it to be there; and I was prepared not to

require any other kind of cause, if he made this clear to me.   98
In the same way I was prepared to ask questions about the sun,
and the moon, and the stars, about their relative speeds, and
revolutions, and changes; and to hear why it is best for each of
them to act and be acted on as they are acted on. I never thought
that, when he said that things are ordered by Mind, he would
introduce any reason for their being as they are, except that they
are best so. I thought that he would assign a cause to each thing,
and a cause to the universe, and then would go on to explain to
me what was best for each thing, and what was the common good
of all. I would not have sold my hopes for a great deal: I seized
the books very eagerly, and read them as fast as I could, in order
that I might know what is best and what is worse.

All my splendid hopes were dashed to the ground, my friend,   XLVII
for as I went on reading I found that the writer made no use of
Mind at all, and that he assigned no causes for the order of things.
His causes were air, and ether, and water, and many other
strange things. I thought that he was exactly like a man who
should begin by saying that Socrates does all that he does by
Mind, and who, when he tried to give a reason for each of my
actions, should say, first, that I am sitting here now, because my
body is composed of bones and muscles, and that the bones are
hard and separated by joints, while the muscles can be tightened
and loosened, and, together with the flesh and the skin which
holds them together, cover the bones; and that therefore, when the
bones are raised in their sockets, the relaxation and contraction
of the muscles make it possible for me now to bend my limbs,
and that that is the cause of my sitting here with my legs bent.
And in the same way he would go on to explain why I am talking
to you: he would assign voice, and air, and hearing, and a
thousand other things as causes; but he would quite forget to
mention the real cause, which is that since the Athenians thought
it right to condemn me, I have thought it right and just to sit
here and to submit to whatever sentence they may think fit to
impose. For, by the dog of Egypt, I think that these muscles
and bones would long ago have been in Megara or Boeotia,   99
prompted by their opinion of what is best, if I had not thought

it better and more honorable to submit to whatever penalty the state inflicts, rather than escape by flight. But to call these things causes is too absurd! If it were said that without bones and muscles and the other parts of my body I could not have carried my resolutions into effect, that would be true. But to say that they are the *cause* of what I do, and that in this way I am acting by Mind, and not from choice of what is best, would be a very loose and careless way of talking. It simply means that a man cannot distinguish the real cause from that without which the cause cannot be the cause, and this it is, I think, which the multitude, groping about in the dark, speaks of as the cause, giving it a name which does not belong to it. And so one man surrounds the earth with a vortex, and makes the heavens sustain it. Another represents the earth as a flat kneading trough, and supports it on a basis of air. But they never think of looking for a power which is involved in these things being disposed as it is best for them to be, nor do they think that such a power has any divine strength. They expect to find an Atlas who is stronger and more immortal and abler to hold the world together, and they never for a moment imagine that it is the binding force of good which really binds and holds things together. I would most gladly learn the nature of that kind of cause from any man, but I wholly failed either to discover it myself or to learn it from anyone else. However, I had a second string to my bow, and perhaps, Cebes, you would like me to describe to you how I proceeded in my search for the cause.

I should like to hear very much indeed, he replied.

XLVIII   When I had given up inquiring into real existence, he proceeded, I thought that I must take care that I did not suffer as people do who look at the sun during an eclipse. For they are apt to lose their eyesight, unless they look at the sun's reflection in water or some such medium. That danger occurred to me. I was afraid that my soul might be completely blinded if I looked at things with my eyes, and tried to grasp them with my senses. So I thought that I must have recourse to conceptions,[14] and

[14] The conception is the imperfect image in man's mind of the self-existing idea, which Plato speaks of in the next chapter. See 74a ff., and *Republic* 507a ff.

examine the truth of existence by means of them. Perhaps my
illustration is not quite accurate. I am scarcely prepared to admit   100
that he who examines existence through conceptions is dealing
with mere reflections, any more than he who examines it as mani-
fested in sensible objects. However, I began in this way. I
assumed in each case whatever principle I judged to be strongest;
and then I held as true whatever seemed to agree with it, whether
in the case of the cause or of anything else, and as untrue whatever seemed not to agree with it. I should like to explain my
meaning more clearly; I don't think you understand me yet.

Indeed I do not very well, said Cebes.

I mean nothing new, he said; only what I have repeated   XLIX
over and over again, both in our conversation today and at other
times. I am going to try to explain to you the kind of cause at
which I have worked, and I will go back to what we have so often
spoken of, and begin with the assumption that there exists an
absolute beauty, and an absolute good, and an absolute greatness, and so on. If you grant me this, and agree that they exist,
I hope to be able to show you what my cause is, and to discover
that the soul is immortal.

You may assume that I grant it you, said Cebes; go on with
your proof.

Then do you agree with me in what follows? he asked. It
appears to me that if anything besides absolute beauty is beautiful,
it is so simply because it partakes of absolute beauty, and I say
the same of all phenomena. Do you allow that kind of cause?

I do, he answered.

Well then, he said, I do no longer recognize nor can I understand these other wise causes: if I am told that anything is beautiful because it has a rich color, or a goodly form, or the like, I
pay no attention, for such language only confuses me; and in a
simple and plain, and perhaps a foolish way, I hold to the doctrine
that the thing is only made beautiful by the presence or communication, or whatever you please to call it, of absolute beauty—I
do not wish to insist on the nature of the communication, but
what I am sure of is, that it is absolute beauty which makes all
beautiful things beautiful. This seems to me to be the safest

answer that I can give myself or others; I believe that I shall never fall if I hold to this; it is a safe answer to make to myself or anyone else, that it is absolute beauty which makes beautiful things beautiful. Don't you think so?

I do.

And it is size that makes large things large, and larger things larger, and smallness that makes smaller things smaller?

Yes.

101 And if you were told that one man was taller than another by a head, and that the shorter man was shorter by a head, you would not accept the statement. You would protest that you say only that the greater is greater by size, and that size is the cause of its being greater; and that the less is only less by smallness, and that smallness is the cause of its being less. You would be afraid to assert that a man is greater or smaller by a head, lest you should be met by the retort, first, that the greater is greater, and the smaller smaller, by the same thing, and secondly, that the greater is greater by a head, which is a small thing, and that it is truly marvelous that a small thing should make a man great. Should you not be afraid of that?

Yes, indeed, said Cebes, laughing.

And you would be afraid to say that ten is more than eight by two, and that two is the cause of the excess; you would say that ten was more than eight by number, and that number is the cause of the excess? And in just the same way you would be afraid to say that a thing two cubits long was longer than a thing one cubit long by half its length, instead of by size, would you not?

Yes, certainly.

Again, you would be careful not to affirm that, if one is added to one, the addition is the cause of two, or, if one is divided, that the division is the cause of two? You would protest loudly that you know of no way in which a thing can be generated, except by participation in its own proper essence; and that you can give no cause for the generation of two except participation in duality; and that all things which are to be two must participate in duality, while whatever is to be one must participate in unity.

You would leave the explanation of these divisions and additions and all such subtleties to wiser men than yourself. You would be frightened, as the saying is, at your own shadow and ignorance, and would·hold fast to the safety of our principle, and so give your answer. But if anyone should attack the principle itself, you would not mind him or answer him until you had considered whether the consequences of it are consistent or inconsistent, and when you had to give an account of the principle itself, you would give it in the same way, by assuming some other principle which you think the strongest of the higher ones, and so go on until you had reached a satisfactory resting place. You would not mix up the first principle and its consequences in your argument, as mere disputants do, if you really wish to discover anything of existence. Such persons will very likely not spend a single word or thought upon that, for they are clever enough to be able to please themselves entirely, though their argument is a chaos. But you, I think, if you are a philosopher, will do as I say. $\quad$ 102

Very true, said Simmias and Cebes together.

Ech. And they were right, Phaedo. I think the clearness of his reasoning, even to the dullest, is quite wonderful.

Phaedo. Indeed, Echecrates, all who were there thought so too.

Ech. So do we who were not there, but who are listening to your story. But how did the argument proceed after that?

Phaedo. They had admitted that each of the Ideas exists $\quad$ L and that Phenomena take the names of the Ideas as they participate in them. Socrates, I think, then went on to ask:

If you say this, do you not, in saying that Simmias is taller than Socrates and shorter than Phaedo, say that Simmias possesses both the attribute of tallness and the attribute of shortness?

I do.

But you admit, he said, that the proposition that Simmias is taller than Socrates is not exactly true, as it is stated; Simmias is not really taller because he is Simmias, but because of his height. Nor again is he taller than Socrates because Socrates is Socrates, but because of Socrates' shortness compared with Simmias' tallness.

True.

Nor is Simmias shorter than Phaedo because Phaedo is Phaedo, but because of Phaedo's tallness compared with Simmias' shortness.

That is so.

Then in this way Simmias is called both short and tall, when he is between the two; he exceeds the shortness of one by the excess of his height, and gives the other a tallness exceeding his own shortness. I daresay you think, he said, smiling, that my language is like a legal document for precision and formality. But I think that it is as I say.

He agreed.

I say it because I want you to think as I do. It seems to me not only that absolute greatness will never be great and small at once, but also that greatness in us never admits smallness, and will not be exceeded. One of two things must happen: either the greater will give way and fly at the approach of its opposite, the less, or it will perish. It will not stand its ground, and receive smallness, and be other than it was, just as I stand my ground, and receive smallness, and remain the very same small man that I was. But greatness cannot endure to be small, being great. Just in the same way again smallness in us will never become nor be great; nor will any opposite, while it remains what it was, become or be at the same time the opposite of what it was. Either it goes away or it perishes in the change.

103
LI

That is exactly what I think, said Cebes.

Thereupon someone—I am not sure who—said,

But surely is not this just the reverse of what we agreed to be true earlier in the argument, that the greater is generated from the less, and the less from the greater, and, in short, that opposites are generated from opposites?[15] But now it seems to be denied that this can ever happen.

Socrates inclined his head to the speaker and listened. Well and bravely remarked, he said, but you have not noticed the difference between the two propositions. What we said then was that a concrete thing is generated from its opposite; what we

[15] 70e ff.

say now is that the absolute opposite can never become opposite to itself, either when it is in us, or when it is in nature. We were speaking then of things in which the opposites are, and we named them after those opposites; but now we are speaking of the opposites themselves, whose inherence gives the things their names; and they, we say, will never be generated from each other. At the same time he turned to Cebes and asked, Did his objection trouble you at all, Cebes?

No, replied Cebes; I don't feel that difficulty. But I will not deny that many other things trouble me.

Then we are quite agreed on this point, he said. An opposite will never be opposite to itself.

No never, he replied.

Now tell me again, he said; do you agree with me in this? LII
Are there not things which you call heat and cold?

Yes.

Are they the same as snow and fire?

No, certainly not.

Heat is different from fire, and cold from snow?

Yes.

But I suppose, as we have said, that you do not think that snow can ever receive heat, and yet remain what it was, snow and hot: it will either retire or perish at the approach of heat.

Certainly.

And fire, again, will either retire or perish at the approach of cold. It will never endure to receive the cold and still remain what it was, fire and cold.

True, he said.

Then, it is true of some of these things that not only the idea itself has a right to its name for all time, but that something else too, which is not the idea, but which has the form of the idea wherever it exists, shares the name. Perhaps my meaning will be clearer by an example. The odd ought always to have the name of odd, ought it not?

Yes, certainly.

Well, my question is this. Is the odd the only thing with this name, or is there something else which is not the same as the odd, 104 but which must always have this name, together with its own, because its nature is such that it is never separated from the odd? There are many examples of what I mean: let us take one of them, the number three, and consider it. Do you not think that we must always call it by the name of odd, as well as by its own name, although the odd is not the same as the number three? Yet the nature of the number three, and of the number five, and of half the whole series of numbers, is such that each of them is odd, though none of them is the same as the odd. In the same way the number two, and the number four, and the whole of the other series of numbers, are each of them always even, though they are not the same as the even. Do you agree or not?

Yes, of course, he replied.

Then see what I want to show you. It is not only opposite ideas which appear not to admit their opposites; things also which are not opposites, but which always contain opposites, seem as if they would not admit the idea which is opposite to the idea that they contain: they either perish or retire at its approach. Shall we not say that the number three would perish or endure anything sooner than become even while it remains three?

Yes, indeed, said Cebes.

And yet, said he, the number two is not the opposite of the number three.

No, certainly not.

Then it is not only the ideas which will not endure the approach of their opposites; there are some other things besides which will not endure such an approach.

LIII   That is quite true, he said.

Shall we determine, if we can, what is their nature? he asked.

Certainly.

Will they not be those things, Cebes, which force whatever they are in to have always not its own idea only, but the idea of some opposite as well?

What do you mean?

Only what we were saying just now. You know, I think, that whatever the idea of three is in, is bound to be not three only, but odd as well.

Certainly.

Well, we say that the opposite idea to the form which produces this result will never come to that thing.

Indeed, no.

But the idea of the odd produces it?

Yes.

And the idea of the even is the opposite of the idea of the odd?

Yes.

Then the idea of the even will never come to three?

Certainly not.

So three has no part in the even?

None.

Then the number three is uneven?

Yes.

So much for the definition which I undertook to give of
things which are not opposites, and yet do not admit opposites;
thus we have seen that the number three does not admit the even,
though it is not the opposite of the even, for it always brings with
it the opposite of the even; and the number two does not admit
the odd, nor fire cold, and so on. Do you agree with me in saying   105
that not only does the opposite not admit the opposite, but also
that whatever brings with it an opposite of anything to which it
goes never admits the opposite of that which it brings? Let me
recall this to you again; there is no harm in repetition. Five will
not admit the idea of the even, nor will the double of five—ten—
admit the idea of the odd. It is not itself an opposite,[16] yet it
will not admit the idea of the odd. Again, one and a half, a half,
and the other numbers of that kind will not admit the idea of the
whole, nor again will such numbers as a third. Do you follow and
agree?

I follow you and entirely agree with you, he said.

Now begin again, and answer me, he said. And imitate me;   LIV
do not answer me in the terms of my question: I mean, do not
give the old safe answer which I have already spoken of, for I see
another way of safety, which is the result of what we have been

---

[16] Reading οὐκ ἐναντίον (Schanz).

saying. If you ask me, what is that which must be in the body to make it hot, I shall not give our old safe and stupid answer, and say that it is heat; I shall make a more refined answer, drawn from what we have been saying, and reply, fire. If you ask me, what is that which must be in the body to make it sick, I shall not say sickness, but fever; and again to the question what is that which must be in number to make it odd, I shall not reply oddness, but unity, and so on. Do you understand my meaning clearly yet?

Yes, quite, he said.

Then, he went on, tell me, what is that which must be in a body to make it alive?

A soul, he replied.

And is this always so?

Of course, he said.

Then the soul always brings life to whatever contains her?

No doubt, he answered.

And is there an opposite to life, or not?

Yes.

What is it?

Death.

And we have already agreed that the soul cannot ever receive the opposite of what she brings?

LV   Yes, certainly we have, said Cebes.

Well; what name did we give to that which does not admit the idea of the even?

The uneven, he replied.

And what do we call that which does not admit justice or music?

The unjust, and the unmusical.

Good; and what do we call that which does not admit death?

The immortal, he said.

And the soul does not admit death?

No.

Then the soul is immortal?

It is.

Good, he said. Shall we say that this is proved? What do you think?

Yes, Socrates, and very sufficiently.

Well, Cebes, he said, if the odd had been necessarily imperishable, must not three have been imperishable?   106

Of course.

And if cold had been necessarily imperishable, snow would have retired safe and unmelted, whenever warmth was applied to it. It would not have perished, and it would not have stayed and admitted the heat.

True, he said.

In the same way, I suppose, if warmth were imperishable, whenever cold attacked fire, the fire would never have been extinguished or have perished. It would have gone away in safety.

Necessarily, he replied.

And must we not say the same of the immortal? he asked. If the immortal is imperishable, the soul cannot perish when death comes upon her. It follows from what we have said that she will not ever admit death, or be in a state of death, any more than three, or the odd itself, will ever be even, or fire, or the heat itself which is in fire, cold. But, it may be said, Granted that the odd does not become even at the approach of the even; why, when the odd has perished, may not the even come into its place? We could not contend in reply that it does not perish, for the uneven is not imperishable; if we had agreed that the uneven was imperishable, we could have easily contended that the odd and three go away at the approach of the even; and we could have urged the same contention about fire and heat and the rest, could we not?

Yes, certainly.

And now, if we are agreed that the immortal is imperishable, then the soul will be not immortal only, but also imperishable; otherwise we shall require another argument.

Nay, he said, there is no need of that, as far as this point goes; for if the immortal, which is eternal, will admit of destruction, what will not?

LVI   And all men would admit, said Socrates, that God, and the essential form of life, and all else that is immortal, never perishes.

All men, indeed, he said; and, what is more, I think, all gods would admit that.

Then if the immortal is indestructible, must not the soul, if it be immortal, be imperishable?

Certainly, it must.

Then, it seems, when death attacks a man, his mortal part dies, but his immortal part retreats before death, and goes away safe and indestructible.

It seems so.

107   Then, Cebes, said he, beyond all question the soul is immortal and imperishable, and our souls will indeed exist in the other world.

I, Socrates, he replied, have no more objections to urge; your reasoning has quite satisfied me. If Simmias, or anyone else, has anything to say, it would be well for him to say it now; for I know not to what other season he can defer the discussion if he wants to say or to hear anything touching this matter.

No, indeed, said Simmias; neither have I any further ground for doubt after what you have said. Yet I cannot help feeling some doubts still in my mind; for the subject of our conversation is a vast one, and I distrust the feebleness of man.

You are right, Simmias, said Socrates, and more than that, you must re-examine our original assumptions, however certain they seem to you; and when you have analyzed them sufficiently, you will, I think, follow the argument, as far as man can follow it; and when that becomes clear to you, you will seek for nothing more.

That is true, he said.

LVII   But then, my friends, said he, we must think of this. If it be true that the soul is immortal, we have to take care of her, not merely on account of the time which we call life, but also on account of all time. Now we can see how terrible is the danger of neglect. For if death had been a release from all things, it would have been a godsend to the wicked; for when they died they would have been released with their souls from the body and

from their own wickedness. But now we have found that the
soul is immortal, and so her only refuge and salvation from evil
is to become. as perfect and wise as possible. For she takes
nothing with her to the other world but her education and culture;
and these, it is said, are of the greatest service or of the greatest
injury to the dead man at the very beginning of his journey
thither. For it is said that the genius, who has had charge of
each man in his life, proceeds to lead him, when he is dead, to
a certain place where the departed have to assemble and receive
judgment and then go to the world below with the guide who
is appointed to conduct them thither. And when they have received
their deserts there, and remained the appointed time, another
guide brings them back again after many long revolutions of
ages. So this journey is not as Aeschylus describes it in the
Telephus, where he says that "a simple way leads to Hades." 108
But I think that the way is neither simple nor single; there would
have been no need of guides had it been so; for no one could
miss the way if there were but one path. But this road must
have many branches and many windings, as I judge from the
rites of burial on earth.[17] The orderly and wise soul follows her
leader and is not ignorant of the things of that world; but
the soul which lusts after the body flutters about the body and
the visible world for a long time, as I have said, and struggles
hard and painfully, and at last is forcibly and reluctantly dragged
away by her appointed genius. And when she comes to the
place where the other souls are, if she is impure and stained
with evil, and has been concerned in foul murders, or if she has
committed any other crimes that are akin to these and the deeds
of kindred souls, then everyone shuns her and turns aside from
meeting her, and will neither be her companion nor her guide,
and she wanders about by herself in extreme distress until a
certain time is completed, and then she is borne away by force
to the habitation which befits her. But the soul that has spent
her life in purity and temperance has the gods for her companions and guides, and dwells in the place which befits her.

[17] Sacrifices were offered to the gods of the lower world in places where
three roads met.

There are many wonderful places in the earth; and neither its nature nor its size is what those who are wont to describe it imagine, as a friend has convinced me.

LVIII What do you mean, Socrates? said Simmias. I have heard a great deal about the earth myself, but I have never heard the view of which you are convinced. I should like to hear it very much.

Well, Simmias, I don't think that it needs the skill of Glaucus to describe it to you, but I think that it is beyond the skill of Glaucus to prove it true. I am sure that I could not do so; and besides, Simmias, even if I knew how, I think that my life would come to an end before the argument was finished. But there is nothing to prevent my describing to you what I believe to be the form of the earth and its regions.

Well, said Simmias, that will do.

In the first place then, said he, I believe that the earth is a spherical body placed in the center of the heavens, and that therefore it has no need of air or of any other force to support
109 it; the equiformity of the heavens in all their parts, and the equipoise of the earth itself, are sufficient to hold it up. A thing in equipoise placed in the center of what is equiform cannot incline in any direction, either more or less; it will remain unmoved and in perfect balance. That, said he, is the first thing that I believe.

And rightly, said Simmias.

Also, he proceeded, I think that the earth is of vast extent, and that we who dwell between the Phasis and the pillars of Heracles inhabit only a small portion of it, and dwell round the sea, like ants or frogs round a marsh; and I believe that many other men dwell elsewhere in similar places. For everywhere on the earth there are many hollows of every kind of shape and size, into which the water and the mist and the air collect; but the earth itself lies pure in the purity of the heavens, wherein are the stars, and which men who speak of these things commonly call ether. The water and the mist and the air, which collect into the hollows of the earth, are the sediment of it. Now we dwell in these hollows though we think that we are dwelling on the surface of the earth. We are just like a man dwelling in the depths of the ocean who thought that he was dwelling on its surface and believed that the sea was the heaven, because he saw the sun and the stars through the water; but who was too weak and slow ever to have reached the water's surface, and to have lifted his head from the sea, and come out from his depths to our world, and seen, or heard from one who had seen, how much purer and fairer our world was than the place wherein he dwelt. We are just in that state; we dwell in a hollow of the earth, and think that we are dwelling on its surface; and we call the air heaven, and think it to be the heaven wherein the stars run their courses. But the truth is that we are too weak and slow to pass through to the surface of the air.[18] For if any man could reach the surface, or take wings and fly upward, he would look up and see a world beyond, just as the fishes look forth from the sea, and behold our world. And he would know that that was the real heaven, and the real light, and the real earth, 110 if his nature were able to endure the sight. For this earth, and its stones, and all its regions have been spoiled and corroded, as things in the sea are corroded by the brine: nothing of any worth grows in the sea, nor, in short, is there anything therein without blemish, but, wherever land does exist, there are only caves, and sand, and vast tracts of mud and slime, which are not worthy even to be compared with the fair things of our world. But you would think that the things of that other world still further surpass the things of our world. I can tell you a tale, Simmias, about what is on the earth that lies beneath the heavens, which is worth your hearing.

Indeed, Socrates, said Simmias, we should like to hear your tale very much.

Well, my friend, he said, this is my tale. In the first place, LIX the earth itself, if a man could look at it from above, is like one of those balls which are covered with twelve pieces of leather, and is marked with various colors, of which the colors that our painters use here are, as it were, samples. But there the whole earth is covered with them, and with others which are far brighter and purer ones than they. For part of it is purple of marvelous

[18] Omitting εἶναι αὐτόν (Schanz).

beauty, and part of it is golden, and the white of it is whiter than chalk or snow. It is made up of the other colors in the same way, and also of colors which are more beautiful than any that we have ever seen. The very hollows in it, that are filled with water and air, have themselves a kind of color, and glisten amid the diversity of the others, so that its form appears as one unbroken and varied surface. And what grows in this fair earth —its trees and flowers and fruit—is more beautiful than what grows with us in the same proportion; and so likewise are the hills and the stones in their smoothness and transparency and color. The pebbles which we prize in this world, our cornelians, and jaspers, and emeralds, and the like, are but fragments of them, but there all the stones are as our precious stones, and even more beautiful still. The reason of this is that they are pure and not corroded or spoiled, as ours are, with the decay and brine from the sediment that collects in the hollows and brings to the stones and the earth and all animals and plants deformity and disease.

111 All these things, and with them gold and silver and the like, adorn the real earth; and they are conspicuous from their multitude and size, and the many places where they are found; so that he who could behold it would be a happy man. Many creatures live upon it; and there are men, some dwelling inland, and others round the air, as we dwell round the sea, and others in islands encircled by the air, which lie near the continent. In a word, they use the air as we use water and the sea, and the ether as we use the air. The temperature of their seasons is such that they are free from disease, and live much longer than we do; and in sight, and hearing, and smell, and the other senses, they are as much more perfect than we, as air is purer than water, and ether than air. Moreover, they have sanctuaries and temples of the gods, in which the gods dwell in very truth; they hear the voices and oracles of the gods, and see them in visions, and have intercourse with them face to face; and they see the sun and moon and stars as they really are; and in other matters their happiness is of a piece with this.

LX   That is the nature of the earth as a whole, and of what is upon it; and everywhere on its globe there are many regions in

the hollows, some of them deeper and more open than that in which we dwell; and others also deeper, but with narrower mouths; and others again shallower and broader than ours. All these are connected by many channels beneath the earth, some of them narrow and others wide; and there are passages by which much water flows from one of them to another, as into basins, and vast and never-failing rivers of both hot and cold water beneath the earth, and much fire, and great rivers of fire, and many rivers of liquid mud, some clearer and others more turbid, like the rivers of mud which precede the lava stream in Sicily, and the lava stream itself. These fill each hollow in turn, as each stream flows round to it. All of them are moved up and down by a certain oscillation which is in the earth and which is produced by a natural cause of the following kind. One of the chasms in the earth is larger than all the others, and pierces right through it, from side to side. Homer describes it in the   112
words—

Far away, where is the deepest depth beneath the earth.[19]

And elsewhere he and many others of the poets have called it Tartarus. All the rivers flow into this chasm and out of it again; and each of them comes to be like the soil through which it flows. The reason why they all flow into and out of the chasm is that the liquid has no bottom or base to rest on; it oscillates and surges up and down, and the air and wind around it do the same, for they accompany it in its passage to the other side of the earth, and in its return; and just as in breathing the breath is always in process of being exhaled and inhaled, so there the wind, oscillating with the water, produces terrible and irresistible blasts as it comes in and goes out. When the water retires with a rush to what we call the lower parts of the earth, it flows through to the regions of those streams and fills them, as if it were pumped into them. And again, when it rushes back hither from those regions, it fills the streams here again, and then they flow through the channels of the earth and make their way to their

[19] *Iliad* VIII. 14.

several places, and create seas, and lakes, and rivers, and springs.
Then they sink once more into the earth, and after making, some
a long circuit through many regions, and some a shorter one
through fewer, they fall again into Tartarus, some at a point
much lower than that at which they rose, and others only a little
lower; but they all flow in below their point of issue. And some
of them burst forth again on the side on which they entered;
others again on the opposite side; and there are some which
completely encircle the earth, twining round it, like snakes, once
or perhaps oftener, and then fall again into Tartarus, as low down
as they can. They can descend as far as the center of the earth
from either side but no farther. Beyond that point on either
side they would have to flow uphill.

LXI   These streams are many, and great, and various; but among
them all are four, of which the greatest and outermost, which
flows round the whole of the earth, is called Oceanus. Opposite
Oceanus, and flowing in the reverse direction, is Acheron, which
113   runs through desert places and then under the earth until it
reaches the Acherusian lake, whither the souls of the dead generally
go, and after abiding there the appointed time, which for some
is longer and for others shorter, are sent forth again to be born
as animals. The third river rises between these two, and near
its source falls into a vast and fiery region and forms a lake
larger than our sea, seething with water and mud. Thence it goes
forth turbid and muddy round the earth, and after many windings comes to the end of the Acherusian lake, but it does not
mingle with the waters of the lake; and after many windings
more beneath the earth, it falls into the lower part of Tartarus.
This is the river that men name Pyriphlegethon; and portions of
it are discharged in the lava streams, wherever they are found on
the earth. The fourth river is on the opposite side; it is said to
fall first into a terrible and savage region, of which the color is
one dark blue. It is called the Stygian stream, and the lake which
its waters create is called Styx. After falling into the lake and
receiving strange powers in its waters, it sinks into the earth,
and runs winding about in the opposite direction to Pyriphlegethon,
which it meets in the Acherusian lake from the opposite side.

Its waters, too, mingle with no other waters; it flows round in a circle and falls into Tartarus opposite to Pyriphlegethon. Its name, the poets say, is Cocytus.

Such is the nature of these regions; and when the dead come to the place whither each is brought by his genius, sentence is first passed on them according as their lives have been good and holy, or not. Those whose lives seem to have been neither very good nor very bad go to the river Acheron, and, embarking on the vessels which they find there, proceed to the lake. There they dwell, and are punished for the crimes which they have committed, and are purified and absolved; and for their good deeds they are rewarded, each according to his deserts. But all who appear to be incurable from the enormity of their sins—those who have committed many and great sacrileges, and foul and lawless murders, or other crimes like these—are hurled down to Tartarus by the fate which is their due, whence they never come forth again. Those who have committed sins which are great, but not too great for atonement, such, for instance, as those who have used violence toward a father or a mother in wrath and then repented of it for the rest of their lives, or who have committed homicide in some similar way, have also to descend into Tartarus; but then when they have been there a year, a wave casts them forth, the homicides by Cocytus, and the parricides and matricides by Pyriphlegethon; and when they have been carried as far as the Acherusian lake they cry out and call on those whom they slew or outraged, and beseech and pray that they may be allowed to come out into the lake, and be received as comrades. And if they prevail, they come out, and their sufferings cease; but if they do not, they are carried back to Tartarus, and thence into the rivers again, and their punishment does not end until they have prevailed on those whom they wronged: such is the sentence pronounced on them by their judges. But such as have been pre-eminent for holiness in their lives are set free and released from this world, as from a prison; they ascend to their pure habitation and dwell on the earth's surface. And those of them who have sufficiently purified themselves with philosophy live thenceforth without bodies and proceed to dwellings still fairer than these, which are not easily described, and of which I have not time to speak now.[20] But for all these reasons, Simmias, we must leave nothing undone, that we may obtain virtue and wisdom in this life. Noble is the prize, and great the hope.

LXIII   A man of sense will not insist that these things are exactly as I have described them. But I think that he will believe that something of the kind is true of the soul and her habitations, seeing that she is shown to be immortal, and that it is worth his while to stake everything on this belief. The venture is a fair one, and he must charm his doubts with spells like these. That is why I have been prolonging the fable all this time. For these reasons a man should be of good cheer about his soul if in his life he has renounced the pleasures and adornments of the body, because they were nothing to him, and because he thought that they would do him not good but harm; and if he has instead earnestly pursued the pleasures of learning, and adorned his soul with the adornment of temperance, and justice, and courage, and

115   freedom, and truth, which belongs to her and is her own, and so awaits his journey to the other world, in readiness to set forth whenever fate calls him. You, Simmias and Cebes, and the rest will set forth at some future day, each at his own time. But me now, as a tragic poet would say, fate calls at once; and it is time for me to betake myself to the bath. I think that I had better bathe before I drink the poison, and not give the women the trouble of washing my dead body.

LXIV   When he had finished speaking Crito said, Be it so, Socrates. But have you any commands for your friends or for me about your children, or about other things? How shall we serve you best?

Simply by doing what I always tell you, Crito. Take care of your own selves, and you will serve me and mine and yourselves in all that you do, even though you make no promises now. But if you are careless of your own selves, and will not follow the

---

[20] The account of the rewards and punishments of the next world given in *Republic* X. 614b ff., the story of Er the son of Armenius, is worth comparing with the preceding passage.

path of life which we have pointed out in our discussions both
today and at other times, all your promises now, however profuse
and earnest they are, will be of no avail.

We will do our best, said Crito. But how shall we bury
you?

As you please, he answered; only you must catch me first
and not let me escape you. And then he looked at us with a
smile and said, My friends, I cannot convince Crito that I am
the Socrates who has been conversing with you and arranging
his arguments in order. He thinks that I am the body which
he will presently see a corpse, and he asks how he is to bury me.
All the arguments which I have used to prove that I shall not
remain with you after I have drunk the poison, but that I shall
go away to the happiness of the blessed, with which I tried to
comfort you and myself, have been thrown away on him. Do
you therefore be my sureties to him, as he was my surety at the
trial, but in a different way. He was surety for me then that I
would remain; but you must be my sureties to him that I shall
go away when I am dead, and not remain with you; then he
will feel my death less; and when he sees my body being burned
or buried, he will not be grieved because he thinks that I am
suffering dreadful things; and at my funeral he will not say
that it is Socrates whom he is laying out, or bearing to the grave,
or burying. For, dear Crito, he continued, you must know that
to use words wrongly is not only a fault in itself, it also creates
evil in the soul. You must be of good cheer, and say that you
are burying my body; and you may bury it as you please and 116
as you think right.

With these words he rose and went into another room to LXV
bathe. Crito went with him and told us to wait. So we waited,
talking of the argument and discussing it, and then again dwelling
on the greatness of the calamity which had fallen upon us: it
seemed as if we were going to lose a father and to be orphans
for the rest of our life. When he had bathed, and his children
had been brought to him—he had two sons quite little, and one
grown up—and the women of his family were come, he spoke

with them in Crito's presence, and gave them his last instruc-
tions; then he sent the women and children away and returned
to us. By that time it was near the hour of sunset, for he had
been a long while within. When he came back to us from the
bath he sat down, but not much was said after that. Presently
the servant of the Eleven came and stood before him and said,
"I know that I shall not find you unreasonable like other men,
Socrates. They are angry with me and curse me when I bid them
drink the poison because the authorities make me do it. But I
have found you all along the noblest and gentlest and best man
that has ever come here; and now I am sure that you will not
be angry with me, but with those who you know are to blame.
And so farewell, and try to bear what must be as lightly as you
can; you know why I have come." With that he turned away
weeping, and went out.

Socrates looked up at him and replied, Farewell, I will do
as you say. Then he turned to us and said, How courteous the
man is! And the whole time that I have been here, he has
constantly come in to see me, and sometimes he has talked to me,
and has been the best of men; and now, how generously he weeps
for me! Come, Crito, let us obey him; let the poison be brought
if it is ready, and if it is not ready, let it be prepared.

Crito replied: But, Socrates, I think that the sun is still upon
the hills; it has not set. Besides, I know that other men take
the poison quite late, and eat and drink heartily, and even enjoy
the company of their chosen friends, after the announcement
has been made. So do not hurry; there is still time.

Socrates replied: And those whom you speak of, Crito,
naturally do so, for they think that they will be gainers by so
doing. And I naturally shall not do so, for I think that I should
117   gain nothing by drinking the poison a little later, but my own
contempt for so greedily saving a life which is already spent. So
do not refuse to do as I say.

LXVI   Then Crito made a sign to his slave who was standing by;
and the slave went out, and after some delay returned with the
man who was to give the poison, carrying it prepared in a cup.

When Socrates saw him, he asked, You understand these things, my good man, what have I to do?

You have only to drink this, he replied, and to walk about until your legs feel heavy, and then lie down; and it will act of itself. With that he handed the cup to Socrates, who took it quite cheerfully, Echecrates, without trembling, and without any change of color or of feature, and looked up at the man with that fixed glance of his, and asked, What say you to making a libation from this draught? May I, or not? We only prepare so much as we think sufficient, Socrates, he answered. I understand, said Socrates. But I suppose that I may, and must, pray to the gods that my journey hence may be prosperous. That is my prayer; may it be so. With these words he put the cup to his lips and drank the poison quite calmly and cheerfully. Till then most of us had been able to control our grief fairly well; but when we saw him drinking and then the poison finished, we could do so no longer: my tears came fast in spite of myself, and I covered my face and wept for myself; it was not for him, but at my own misfortune in losing such a friend. Even before that Crito had been unable to restrain his tears, and had gone away; and Apollodorus, who had never once ceased weeping the whole time, burst into a loud wail and made us one and all break down by his sobbing except Socrates himself. What are you doing, my friends? he exclaimed. I sent away the women chiefly in order that they might not behave in this way; for I have heard that a man should die in silence. So calm yourselves and bear up. When we heard that, we were ashamed, and we ceased from weeping. But he walked about, until he said that his legs were getting heavy, and then he lay down on his back, as he was told. And the man who gave the poison began to examine his feet and legs from time to time. Then he pressed his foot hard and asked if there was any feeling in it, and Socrates said, No; and then his legs, and so higher and higher,   118 and showed us that he was cold and stiff. And Socrates felt himself and said that when it came to his heart, he should be gone. He was already growing cold about the groin, when he uncovered his face, which had been covered, and spoke for the last time.

Crito, he said, I owe a cock to Asclepius; do not forget to pay it.[21] It shall be done, replied Crito. Is there anything else that you wish? He made no answer to this question; but after a short interval there was a movement, and the man uncovered him, and his eyes were fixed. Then Crito closed his mouth and his eyes.

Such was the end, Echecrates, of our friend, a man, I think, who was the wisest and justest, and the best man I have ever known.

---

[21] These words probably refer to the offering usually made to Asclepius on recovery from illness. Death is a release from the "fitful fever of life." See, for instance 66b ff., 67c. Another explanation is to make the word refer to the omission of a trifling religious duty.